AF538938

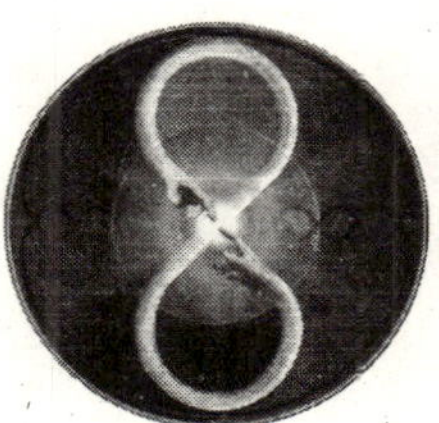

The Life after Death

Born, to be born again...

(TRANSMIGRATION)

Ramanuj Prasad

PUSTAK MAHAL®

Publishers
Pustak Mahal®

J-3/16 , Daryaganj, New Delhi-110002
☎ 23276539, 23272783, 23272784 • *Fax:* 011-23260518
E-mail: info@pustakmahal.com • *Website:* www.pustakmahal.com

Sales Centre

- 10-B, Netaji Subhash Marg, Daryaganj, New Delhi-110002
  ☎ 23268292, 23268293, 23279900 • *Fax:* 011-23280567
  E-mail: rapidexdelhi@indiatimes.com
- 6686, Khari Baoli, Delhi-110006
  ☎ 23944314, 23911979

Branches

Bengaluru: ☎ 080-22234025 • *Telefax:* 080-22240209
E-mail: pustak@airtelmail.in • pustak@sancharnet.in
Mumbai: ☎ 022-22010941, 022-22053387
E-mail: rapidex@bom5.vsnl.net.in
Patna: ☎ 0612-3294193 • *Telefax:* 0612-2302719
E-mail: rapidexptn@rediffmail.com
Hyderabad: *Telefax:* 040-24737290
E-mail: pustakmahalhyd@yahoo.co.in

ISBN 978-81-223-0917-1

Edition: 2012

Printed at : **Glorious Printers Delhi**

Dedication

"A flower on the
lotus feet of
the Lord of senses

—Hṛśīkeśa"

Invocation

पुनरपि जननं पुनरपि मरणं
    पुनरपि जननी जठरे शयनम
इह संसारे बहुदुस्तारे
    कृपया पारे पाहि मुरारे
        भज गोविन्दं

Birth unceasing! Death unceasing!
    Ever to pass through a mother's womb!
Hard to cross the world's wide ocean;
    Lord, redeem me through thy mercy!
        Worship the Lord

Transliteration of Devanāgarī

अ	a	क	k	ट	ṭ	प	p	ष	ṣ
आ	ā	ख	kh	ठ	ṭh	फ	ph	स	s
इ	I	ग	g	ड	ḍ	ब	b	ह	ḥ
ई	ī	घ	gh	ढ	ḍh	भ	bh		
उ	u	ङ	ń	ण	ṇ	म	m		
ऊ	ū	च	c	त	t	य	y		
ऋ	ṛ	छ	ch	थ	th	र	r		
ए	e	ज	j	द	d	ल	l		
ऐ	ai	झ	jh	ध	dh	व	v		
ओ	o	ञ	ñ	न	n	श	ś		
औ	au								

List of Abbreviations

1.	BG	Bhagawad-Gīta
2.	Bh.	Bhāgavata Purāṇa
3.	Br.	Bṛhadāraṇyaka Upaniṣad
4.	Br. Vvp.	Brahmavaivarta Purāṇa
5.	G. Purāṇa	Garuda Purāṇa
6.	PP.	Padma Purāṇa
7.	Tai.	Taittrīya Upaniṣad
8.	Kaṭha	Kaṭhopaniṣad
9.	Kena	Kenopaniṣad

Contents

Introduction

जातस्य हि ध्रुवो मृत्युर्ध्रुवं जन्म मृतस्य च ।
तस्मादपरिहार्येऽर्थे न त्वं शोचितुमर्हसि ॥

"Death is certain of that which is born; birth is certain of that which is dead. You should not, therefore, lament over the inevitable". —*B.G.2-27*

When a body evades functioning properly and it disintegrates into its constituent elements, this modification is called death. But when other body crops up from the same matter, it is the birth that contains the inherent propelling force known by the name **'the desires'**, which drive upon to the mundane activities of the life again. The birth and death are the two points on the circumference of the wheel of the universe. Our wholesome is limited in between these two points, nothing beyond; and if anything beyond these two points exists, that is unknown or speculative, if we do not base our understanding through the eyes of the scriptural truth.

The nihilism professes that an individual retains his individuality as long as the operative force exists and this so called individuality makes sense through birth and death. After burning away the oil of *karma*, the flame goes off, that is the end of the cycle and is also the end of the man. The school of atheists makes its point of view on birth and death as the natural phenomena of modifications, compared with a lump of clay in the rivers. Body is assumed to undergo the change, the change which is inherent in the body, the body is matter and matter continues to be in a flux of modification.

However, the birth and death are serious matters and its mystery has been debated in the past and shall continue to be the subject in future also; it exists even in the present as the existence of future depends upon the present. Some people avoid talking about death, as they are afraid to face the fact of life. The hare avoids seeing the danger, rather thrusts its head in the bush to assure itself of safety.

Everyday thousands of people die but we do not think for a moment that we too shall die. We continue with our routine without being affected by it. This was the wisdom that exposed the human thoughts through Dharmaputra *Yudhishtira* in his reply to *Yakṣa.* One of the questions put by *Yakṣa to Yudhishtira* was "What is the most wonderful thing in the world"? The answer of *Yudhishtira* was this: "Everyday and day after day, many human beings die. But we do not think of death; we think that we shall never die. What can be more wonderful than this?"

Some believe that death is evil and Satan is the author of it. However, let us take that death brings the end of the journey to one of the places, so it is not full stop but only a comma. According to science, there are two kinds of death, one is the conscious life and the other one is the organic or cellular life, which does not depend on the former. Death lives with all its mysteries and its sacredness. We are not in the least able to present what life is, still less what death is when we probe into different conditions such as coma, stoppage of heart beat, stoppage of pulse or respiration. But final word of science about death is the decomposition and putrefaction as we have come across the cases of premature burial and embalming, recorded in medical journals of the world for loss or suspension of conscious. So the law is made for burial only after decomposition is set in.

It is also believed that the sources of consciousness and mind are indestructible, so is also life. Life is indestructible in light of life force, the *prāṇa.* It is the macro *prāṇa* that was placed as micro. Micro joined the macro. The validity depends upon meaning of death. There is no meaning in praying for everlasting peace unless there is continuity of existence even after death, which is the central theme of dialogue between the student Nāciketas and the teacher – the Lord of death himself.

The present life has justification to the extent that it succeeds in breaking the bondage. The embodied soul goes on moving from one body to another till its release, when it requires no more experiences. It is to discover that it knows everything that has to be known, thus the death is the process of enrichment through change for better. The birth and death is the scheme of existence and attainment. In spiritual span, it teaches the great lesson of detachment.

Transmigration presupposes the existence of soul. What about the body that it takes one after another? Body is the matter that cannot be created or destroyed but subject to modifications only. There is no significance to the body without the soul and thus the soul is the cause for the existence of the body. Cause is always present in the effect – the body, before, during and after, just as the clay in the pot. All the bodies that come into manifestation must be available in unmanifest form at the disposal of the soul for use at its descent, which means that the soul itself makes available the body it wants according to its choice, governed by the law of *karma. Vedānta* teaches that one should prepare oneself through enquiry, the remedy against fear of death, thus a fulfilment, not destruction, where a spiritually developed person departs – his passing is easy and smooth, whereas an undeveloped person undergoes fear, shock and agony. Though the dying person appears unconscious outwardly, he is fully conscious inwardly and experiences transition from the present life to the next.

The transmigration is a conjunction of two separate entities – the body [matter] and the soul [spirit] and how they stand related with each other is revealed herewith:

"It [self] is not born and it does not die at any time. And the spirit does not again come into existence by being born. The Ātma itself is birth less, constant, eternal and ancient; it is not slain, when the body is slain".

"Just as a person gives up worn out clothes and puts on other new cloth even so does the embodied self give up decrepit bodies and enter other new ones".

The crest in this relationship is the pre and post-existence of the soul; the bodies undergo the modification, not the soul at any point of time; that it is beyond time.

The author records his sincere and profound gratitude to Sri G. Ramamurthy, for the invaluable help and assistance that he afforded in this work, without any reservation.

CHAPTER I

Eternal Presence

CHAPTER I

Eternal Presence

Eastern Thoughts and Beliefs (Part-I)

Śruti: This verse of *Kaṭhopaniṣad* is so direct and simple that it is hardly seen elsewhere. It says "If here [in this life] one is able to comprehend Him [Brahman] before the death of the body, he will be liberated from the bondage of the world; if one is not able to comprehend Him, then he has to take a body again in the world of creation". *Kaṭha* VI – IV

The above statement is also pregnant with the idea that the death is for the body only. Now let us see what *Kenopaniṣad* says: "If one knows [that Brahman] here [i.e. in this world] then the true end [of all human aspirations] is [gained]. If one knows not [that] here, great is the destruction".

—*Kena* II-V

The destruction is indicative of birth and death in varying *lokas* [*yoni*] and thus the miseries of *samsāra* that is pain and pleasure and modifications of the mortal body. Therefore, it is imperative to realize the Brahman, i.e. oneness of the Self or the unity of *Ātman* in all and become immortal, indicating to become Brahman itself. Becoming is not in the literal sense but means 'as though' which means knowing is becoming.

The third illustration has been taken to highlight the technical terms in five oblations, discussed in Chapter III. "There is one Supreme Self in the midst of this universe. He himself is the fire that is fully established in the water [body]. By knowing Him alone one goes beyond death, there is no other path to go by". He only, who is capable of destroying the cause of bondage, will attain liberation. Here the universe signifies earth, heaven and all the intermediary space. He is fire because He burns the ignorance. He is subtle in the water that formed the body. Thus it is said, "Thus indeed after the fifth oblation, the water comes to be called a person. The salibe in the heart was made pure like clear water by sacrifice and charity. ['Thou art That' is the idea].

Smṛti [Bhagavad-Gīta]

The blessed Lord said, *"Many are the births taken by me and you, O Arjuna! I know them all while you know not O! Partha"*.

The bound souls are born to work out their *karma*, whereas the Lord is beyond *karma*. Here the *Jīva* is Arjuna in this context.

The ninth verse of this fourth chapter says: *"He who knows My divine birth and action in true light, having dropped the body, comes not again but comes unto Me; O Arjuna"*.

The unborn *Īśvara* puts on the appearance of birth and growth by His divine power that is the actionless entity, stages holy activities for the good of the world. These pure personalities, who understand these facts about the Lord, live in the world unaffected and after the fall of the body return not, they attain liberation from the cycle of birth and death.

Purāṇas: What is the view of the Purāṇas on the issue of the transmigration of the soul?

The foundation of the *Purāṇas* rests on this very concept. All legends progress through rebound, reactions and rebirth. The rebirth, hell and heaven are the instruments with which *Purāṇas* operate to discipline the life style of the individual and groups. Therefore, *Purāṇas* without the concept of rebirth, that is transmigration, is difficult to conceive even. For example, Jaya and Vijaya of the *devaloka* descended on the earth as Hiraṇyākṣa – Hiraṇyakaṣipu and Rāvaṇa – Kumbhakarṇa. Mother Sati herself had reincarnation as Pārvatī. We may see some excerpts from Purāṇas in later pages.

Cāruvākas

Cāruvākas, the materialist philosophy fails to admit of the supernatural power being [god] and their impartiality as they do not see [direct perception] and, therefore, concludes that nothing exists after the death of the body. *Karma* is inoperative and a mere illusion. Everything is derived from the elements and that is the inherent force. Direct perception gives true knowledge and accordingly the *Vedas* cannot be a valid source of knowledge. The life is meant to get maximum pleasures. Cāruvākas accept only four elements, as ether cannot be seen. Consciousness is mere product of matter. When matter is arranged in a particular order, the Consciousness emerged, showing sign of life in the body. Cāruvākas deny the existentce of soul – *Ātma* as surviving or transmigrating. They deny the past and future births. It is also not accepted that foetus is endowed with Consciousness.

The materialist, Ajita denounced moral values.

"There is no such thing as alms or sacrifice or offering. There is neither fruit nor result of good or evil deeds. There is no such thing as this world or the next. There is neither father nor mother, nor beings springing into life without them. There are in the world no recluses or Brahmins who have reached the highest point, who walk perfectly, and who, having understood and realized, by themselves alone, both this world and the next, make their wisdom known to others."

Pūrana Kassapa taught a theory of non-action [*akriya*]. He argued that however bad a deed a man might do, he did not commit sin.

"To him who acts or causes another to act, to him who mutilates or causes to mutilate, to him who punishes or causes another to punish, to him who causes grief or torment, to him who trembles or causes others to tremble, to him who kills a living creature, who takes what is not given, who breaks into houses, who commits robbery, or dacoity, or highway robbery, or adultery, or who speaks lies, to him thus acting there is no guilt. If with a discus with an edge sharp as a razor he should make all the living creatures on the earth one heap, one mass of flesh there would be no guilt thence resulting, no increase of guilt would ensue."

However good an action a man may perform, he cannot acquire merit. 'In generosity, in self-mastery, in control of the senses, in speaking truth there is neither merit nor increase of merit'.

'Were he to go along the south bank of the Ganges striking and slaying, mutilating and having men mutilated, oppressing and having men oppressed, there would be no guilt thence resulting, no increase of guilt would ensue. Were he to go along the north bank of Ganges giving alms and ordering gifts to be given, offering sacrifices or causing them to be offered, there would be no merit thence resulting, no increase of merit.'

Another well-known materialist was Bṛhaspati [date unknown]. He is said to have composed a nihilistic work [*sūtra*], which has perished. A poem ascribed to him denouncing the priests runs as follows:

> 'No heaven exists, no final liberation,
> No soul, no other world, no rites of caste,......
> The triple Veda, triple self-command,
> And all the dust and ashes of repentance.
> These yield a means of livelihood for men
> Devoid of intellect and manliness.........
> While life endures, let life be spent in ease
> And merriment;
> The costly rites enjoined for those who die
> Are but a means of livelihood devised
> By sacerdotal cunning – nothing more................'

'The three authors of the Vedas were buffoons, knaves, and demons.'

'It is only as a means of livelihood that *Brahmins* have established here all of these ceremonies for the dead'.

'While life remains let a man live happily, let him feed on ghee even though he runs in debt;

When once the body becomes ashes, how can it ever return again?'

Later materialists, also of India, said much the same. The philosopher Gosāla, advocated indeterminism.

'There is no cause, either ultimate or remote, for the depravity [state of being corrupted] of beings; they become depraved without reason and without any cause. There is no cause, either proximate or remote, for the rectitude of beings; they become pure without reason and without cause. The attainment of any given condition, of any character, does not depend either on one's own acts, or on the acts of another, or human effort. There is no such thing as power or energy, or human strength or human vigor.

'Men are bent this way and that by their fate, by the necessary conditions of the class to which they belong, by their individual nature and it is according to their position in one or other of the six classes that they experience ease or pain'.

[*The materialists' views are the views of the arrogant prejudiced lot, who hide their hatred towards Vedas and brāhmaṇas [the knower of veda]. These arguments are not worth refuting.*}

Jainism

Jainism teaches the aim of life to get detached from desires, which is also the general principle of Hindu scriptures. Though they believe in transmigration of the soul, but their conception of *karma,* which is the governing principle, is different from other philosophies. This, in Jainism, is considered as material which permeates the *Jīvās* throughout its journey and weighing them down to the mundane level, as heat can unite with iron and water with milk, so *Karma* unites with the soul and the soul, so united with *karma* is called soul in bondage, though the way by which it binds is different. As much in the philosophy of Hindus so here also the ideal lies beyond good and evil, so the virtues as well as vices are believed to lead to bondage, though the way by which it binds is different. If through proper self-discipline all *karmas* are worked out, then there arises the full knowledge of Omniscience in the *Jīva,* it becomes free and at last escapes from cycle of death, from bondage of the body, it rises until it reaches the top of the universe, described as *lokākāśa* and there it rests in peaceful bliss for ever. It may not care for worldly affairs thereafter but is certainly not without its own influence for it will serve those that are still struggling to godhead. All liberated souls are gods, once liberated, but may lead even active life but that does not taint him, contrary to others who are entangled even by the unselfish activities [like *Jīvan mukta* of Hinduism].

[*This particular philosophy does not contradict Vedas, though they do not have belief in vedas.*]

Sāṅkhya

Like other systems, that believe in *karma* and transmigration, this philosophy also believes in it, but what transmigrates is not the self because it is all pervading and so does not admit of change of place, but the subtle body [*liṅga śarīra*] consisting the eleven organs of senses along with *buddhi, ahaṁkāra* and the five rudimentary elements [*tanmātras*]. This is a permanent annex so to speak, to each self, which leaves only at release. Death and birth means only the change of the gross body and not of the subtle body. Stored up in the later are all traces of past thoughts and actions. Acquisition of right knowledge depends upon the cleansing of the empirical outfit or more strictly of the *buddhi,* which forms its pre-eminent elements. *Dharma-adharma* are conceived not as the quality of the self but only as modes of *buddhi.* No *Puruṣa* is bound or liberated nor does it migrate. It is *Prakṛti* in its manifold forms that is bound and migrates or liberated.

Buddhism

While *Brahmanism* made 'virtuous conduct' as the means to achieve status in sequence of rebirths of the individual soul, Buddha made his ethical disposition as the means to achieve *'nirvāṇa'* or liberation. Buddha rejected the Brahminic ideal of soul's absorption in the Universal Soul – the Infinite Intelligence. According to Buddhism permanent or Absolute existence is an illusion. Substance and Self, which in Indian philosophy are taken as permanent entities, have received scant attention in Buddhism. In Buddhist's philosophy, change is the main point, which interprets human life in terms of cyclic process involving birth, death and rebirth. The process being continuous and ceaseless is called *'Dharma cakra or Samsāra cakra'.* One who knows and appreciates the mystery of the wheel of life is able to know the truth and avoid ignorance. There is suffering because there is birth. There is birth because there is the will to be reborn. The will to be reborn follows from the desire to cling to the object and because of the desire to enjoy.

According to Buddhists, mind is the sixth sense organ. The death of the living being is not the end; at once another life begins to go through a similar process of birth and death and thus repeats the round of life over and over again. In this way, a living being, when considered in relation to time, forms an endless continuum. The whole series of stages must be taken in their entirety representing the one individual being. Thus, a living being, when regarded in relation to space, forms a complex of five elements although the body is abandoned at death. "Blindness remains as the crystallization of the effects of the actions performed during life". Birth and death are regarded as merely "an abbreviated description of whole life." Repetition of the changes from one form to another is called '*Samsāra*' and Buddhism denies the existence of superior authority – the God.

Buddhists believe in transmigration, but the belief seems to be inconsistent with their denial of an enduring self, some have, therefore, characterized the doctrine as self-contradictory. Deussen, for instance, writes: "This *karman* must have in every case an individual bearer and that is what the *Upaniṣads* call as the *Ātman* and the Buddhists deny, inconsistently deny". But there seems to be no justification for such a criticism. The belief in the *karma* presents no new difficulty to Buddhism, for, if there be action without an agent, there can well be transmigration without transmigrating agent. Further, we have to remember that according to Buddhism, there is transmigration, more precisely rebirth not only at the end of this life as in other schools of thought, but also at every instant. It is not merely one lamp is lit from another, that there is transmigration of light and heat. They are transmitted every moment; only in the former case, a new series of flames are started. Similarly, the *karma* belonging to an 'individual' may transmit itself at death as it does during life; and though the dead person does not revive, another with the same disposition may be born in his stead. If so, it is character as Rhys Davids has put it, "That transmigrates, not any soul or self. When a person dies, his character lives after him and by its force, brings into existence a being, who, though possessing a different form, is entirely influenced by it. And this process will go on until the person in question has completely overcome his thirst for being". If we take this explanation along with what has already been said that self is here recognized as continuity, though not as a unity, we see that there need be no inconsistency in Buddhism upholding the *karma* doctrine. For, it admits both the implications of the doctrine, viz. that nothing that we do, disappear without leaving its result behind and that the good or evil so resulting recoils upon the doer. Buddha conceived of *karma* as an impersonal law in the sphere of morality working according to its nature and by itself.

[*Buddhist's philosophy of transmigration is the transmigration with a difference for want of the agent – the karta, and the karma-phala-dāta.*]

Sri Ramanuja's *Viśiṣta-Dvaita* – Qualified Monism

Ramanuja professes qualitative monism and qualitative pluralism of souls. According to Ramanuja, the birth and death refer only to the souls in association with or disassociation from bodies resulting in contraction and expansion or intelligence. In dissolution or destruction of the world however, the souls become one with a subtle stuff, which does not admit differentiation by name and form. Individual self is a part of higher self. The individual self is the effect of Infinite Intelligence and not a part cut out. The soul is 'knowing subject' as well as an active agent.

Acts [*karma*] belong to the soul and it undergoes the consequence of these acts. So long the souls are bound to bodies, their acts result in bodily consequences but in their state of liberation, unattached to the body, they realize their wishes by mere will. Ramanuja insists on both the individual freedom and divine sovereignty. Ramanuja mentions three classes of souls [*Jīvas*]:

- Eternal and ever free – [*Nitya mukta*].
- Earned freedom through their good actions.
- Those who are still going through the cycle of birth and death.

Some *Viśiṣtadvaitins* can even conceive a fourth category, which is wandering in the *samsāra.* These again go to four divisions: celestial, human, animal and immobile. All the souls are alike, except their bodily differences. Body of the god is the starting point of the process of evolution. It is not created, though undergoes formal change. For Ramanuja, creation is real, so also the world and soul, that every effect pre-exists in its material cause and only the externalization is the implicit form.

Mādhvacārya's-*dvaita*-Dualism

Mādhvacārya comes to qualitative and quantitative plurality of souls. God is the efficient cause and not the material cause. God is guided in His soul-related actions – condemning some and redeeming others – by the *karma* of individuals. We must take note of the *karma* as one's individual's deeds and the *karma* as law of cause and effect [principle phenomena] bringing about the fruits of actions. The individual souls are infinite in number and atomic in size but each one is different from the other, according to the past *karma* and each one is imperfect in its own *way*. All the imperfections of all the souls are on account of its ignorance and sufferings. Mādhva regards the distinction between Brahman and individual soul [*Jīva*] as real and holds that "it is wrong to think that *jīva* and Brahman are not different in release and different in *samsāra*, since two different things at any time cannot become non-different. The soul by nature is conscious and blissful, though subjected to pain and sufferings on account of its connection with material bodies and so long it is not freed from its natural impurities, it is subjected to the cycle of transmigration".

Here also there exist three classifications of souls:

- Eternal free like Śri Lakśmī consort of Nārāyaṇa.
- Those who have freed themselves such as gods, men, sages and ancestors.
- Those who are still bound in bondage.

There are some who are eligible to be released and those who are destined to *samsāra*/hell.

Pūrva Mīmāmsa

According to Pūrva mīmāmsa, one should pursue the goal of dharma and not *mokṣa*, whether as means to an end or an end in itself. This seems to be its aim till a certain stage was reached in the history of the system. In that early period of growth of *mīmāmsa*, only *dharma, artha and kāma* were accepted as human values and not the fourth one, the *mokṣa*. To speak generally, *dharma* is still the highest ideal. But in *Kalpa-Sūtra*, the doctrine in its present form has been practically thrown overboard and replaced it by the ideal of *mokṣa*. This transformation was meant abandonment of many rites taught in the *Vedas*. But the change was more subversive kind in the case of Prabhākara school of thoughts than that of Kumārila. The latter conceived *dharma* as a means to an end and the introduction of *mokṣa* ideal means only the substitution of one to another. If the old aim was the attainment of *svarga*, attainment of some positive good, the new one was *apavarga*, the negative one to escape from *samsāra*. But in the case of the former, which pursued *dharma* as the end, the acceptance of the new ideal means deserting its cherished ideal of doing duty for its own sake and going over completely to the side of Bhattas, for the ideal of *mokṣa* to jump to Sālikanath's description, which is also seeking of an end viz., escape from the trials and travails of *samsāra*. Pūrva mīmāmsa shares the view that *karma* is the cause of bondage and when the cause is removed, the result is restoring the self to its original state. Only those *karmas* are to be abstained from, which are prohibited and optional. The performance of those which give some merits should be pursued and not those which give demerits. These are means for removing the bondage of persons seeking freedom. Even the seeker of freedom should perform the *nitya karma.* It is strictly the insight born out of meditation upon its true nature which is a contributory aid to the freedom doctrine and the name given is *karma-samuchaya vāda.*

Uttara Mīmāmsa – Vedānta

From the point of view of *Vedānta*, the death is compared to going to sleep and after death experiences to dreams. The actions and thoughts of the waking state determine the nature of dreams and likewise the soul reaps the result after death – the life on earth. These experiences may be of the nature as one may call them as heaven or hell. When the soul comes out of sleep, it is rebirth on the earth. It again takes up the thread of life and continues to progress towards its goal. It seems that there is no stop from its upward journey of the soul. However, there is the possibility of detour. After death, experiences, though in the nature of dreams, are tangible and vivid as long as they last.

Similar to the dreamtime, it covers ages. It is also accepted that the rebirth may be directly into a human being without going into higher or lower body compared to the experiences of heaven or hell. *Vedānta* writers have always used analogues and illustrations to explain the points, the subject matter being super-sensuous in nature; there are difficulties in explaining and understanding properly without these techniques. In most of the occasions, these illustrations are from our experiences of daily life, which are easier to understand from known than unknown, from relative truth to Absolute. The unity of Existence, the Consciousness is the foundation, oneness of godhood; the self of man is the self of all beings.

Destiny could not be altered. [That part of the karma which has fructified].

With regard to the nature of our transmigratory existence, Śaṅkarācārya's views are as follows:

The term *karman* has various meanings in Śaṅkara's works and also in other Indian texts. The term *karman* in one aspect means the result of actions, good or bad of the past [experience]. The term *kriyā* seems to be used in the sense of actions, good or bad, which require verbal, physical and mental activities, including the vedic rituals. When Śaṅkara takes up *karman* to discuss its nature and value as the means to final release *[mokṣa]*, he often uses the term synonymously with *kriya* in the sense mentioned above.

Sri Śaṅkara's transmigratory existence seems to consist of the following cycle: 1. *Karmans* or works as the result of actions in the previous existence; 2. one's connection with the body; 3. experience of pleasures and pain; 4. passion and aversion; 5. Actions – kriyā; 6. Merit and demerit [*karmans*]. In other words, the transmigratory existence is the continuously recurring process of the performance of actions [*karman or kriyā*] and experience of their fruits. In this sense, it is possible to replace the above cycle of transmigratory existence by another, i.e. doership [*kartṛtva*] and experiencership [*bhoktṛtva*].

According to them, the transmigratory existence exists as real substance characterized by doership and experiencership. "Even though I exist [externally], still one is not the highest *Ātman* and the nature is transmigratory existence which is characterized by doership and experiencership, since it is dependent on sense-perception and other means of knowledge".

The ultimate cause of this transmigratory existence is *ajñāna* or ignorance *[Upādi*]. In another place, the cycle of transmigratory existence is described as: 1. nescience [*avidya*]; 2. faults [*dośa*]; 3. verbal, physical and mental activities; 4. Accumulation of *Karmans* of which the results are desirable, undesirable and mixed. In this way, transmigratory existence can be traced back to ignorance or nescience. This cycle reminds us of Buddhists theory of dependent origination [*pratītyasamutpāda*], which also has nescience as its factor.

'As knowledge is the very nature of *Ātman*, it is constantly applied figuratively to the intellect. And the absence of discriminating knowledge is beginningless; this and nothing else is conceived to be transmigratory existence'.

'Therefore, transmigratory existence is nothing but nescience due to the absence of discriminating knowledge. For the immovable *Ātman*, transmigratory existence is, as it were, always existent in *Ātman*'.

or

The transmigratory existence is nothing but the absence of discriminating knowledge, concerning *Ātman* and non-*Ātman*. For this reason, final release from transmigratory existence is merely the removal of nescience or cessation of false super-imposition upon *Ātman*, which is by nature ever released, pure, immovable, changeless, immortal and bodiless.

Sri Śaṅkara illustrates as: "as though there is a snake, existing in the rope before there is discrimination, so the transcendentally changeless *Ātman*, this transmigratory existence, though not a reality. Further, Śaṇkara refers to the question: Who is the transmigrator? 'As the seeing is changeless, nor is the reflection, for the reflection is unreal. Nor is the bearer of the 'I'–notion since it is non-conscious. Who could be the transmigrator?'

To this view of transmigratory existence, there is no transmigrator anywhere. Transmigratory existence is unreal. So is the transmigrator. As the immovable *Ātman* exists, it is only regarded as the transmigrator because of nescience.

Note: *This unreality follows from the fact that the very universe is unreal and projection of the Brahman as viewed by the vedantins – the school of Sri Saṅkara.*

Western Thoughts and Beliefs (Part-II)

The School of Pythagoras

Pythagoras was the best-known proponent of transmigration of Greek version. His view: "That the soul is immortal and it is transformed into other kind of living things, further that whenever comes into existence is born again in revolution of a certain as nothing being absolutely new and that all things that are born with life in them ought to be treated as kindred". He cites that there are three types of people; the Olympic game is the characteristic comparison. The type of people who come here are those who come to buy and sell, the second group is that who compete. Best of all are those who come simply to look on. The greatest purification of all is therefore disinterested science and it is the man who devotes himself to that. The true philosopher is he, who has most effectively released himself from the wheel of birth.

Jewish

The treatment of metempsychosis found in the Kalbalah, was limited by the need to confirm to the orthodox scripture and the theory of transmigration was tolerated rather than accepted. The Jewish, therefore, derived mainly from Gnostic, Manichean and Neoplatonic sources, teach that man has absolute free will, but that his soul is tied and sullied by contact with matter. Demon [imperfect] souls try to prevent the fulfilment of finite divine plan. To act out this plan, the spotless souls descend from their original abode in heaven and are incarnated. Punishment and atonement for sins is achieved by another incarnation but before this happens, the now impure soul flits about as a disembodied spirit. If the pious people suffer, it is believed to be for their sins committed in a previous existence. At the end of cycle when all the incarnated souls are once again pure, the *Messianic period* begins.

The soul passes into subsequent body of either human or animal, was the view of Pythagoras, who probably learnt the doctrine in Egypt. The rational mind after having been freed from the chains of the body assumes an ethereal vehicle and passes into the region of the dead where it remains till it is sent back to this world to inhabit some other body of human or animal. After undergoing successive purgation and when sufficiently purified, it is received among the gods and returns back to eternal source from which, it first proceeded. This doctrine was from Judaism until about eighth century, when under the influence of Mohammedan mystics, it was adopted by the Karaites and other Jewish descendants. Saadia, who protested against the belief, mentioned it in Jewish literature.

Socrates

Except in this last point, he resembles Christian martyr or Puritan. In the final passage, he considers what happens after death. It is impossible not to feel that he finally believes in immortality and that he professed uncertainty is only assumed. He is not troubled like the Christian by fear of eternal torment. He has no doubt that his life in the next world would be a happy one. In Phaedo the Polonic Socrates gives reason for the belief in immortality; whether these were the reasons influenced is not known. He maintains that no man sins wittingly and, therefore, only knowledge is needed to make all men perfectly virtuous.

Plato's Theory

On Plato's theory of immortality of soul, Cebes expresses doubt as to the survival of the soul after death and the arguments offered by Socrates are poor.

- All things, which have opposites, are generated from their opposites. As such, as life and death are opposite to each other, therefore, each must generate the other. It follows that the soul of the dead exists somewhere and comes back to earth in due course. St. Paul's statement is "the seed is not quickened except it due".

- That knowledge is recollection and, therefore, the soul must have existed before birth. The theory that knowledge is recollection is supported and based on "that we have idea such as exact equality which cannot be derived from experience. We have experience of approximate equality but absolute equality is never found among sensible objects and yet we know what we mean by 'absolute equality' Since we have not had it from experience, we must have brought the knowledge with us form previous existence. thus the existence.

- Essences and our capacity to apprehend them prove the pre-existence of the soul with knowledge. "There is no teaching but recollection".

This conclusion is drawn in the Meno as in the Phaeda that knowledge is brought by the soul from previous existence.

The doctrine of reminiscence is considered as established. Cebes says about half of what is required has been proved to wit that our soul existed before we were born – "that the soul will exist after death as well as before birth is the other half of which the proof is still wanting".

Socrates applies to this as "everything is being generated from its opposites", so the death must generate life just as much as life generates death. It is further added that what is complex can be dissolved and that the soul, like the ideas is simple and not compounded of parts. What is simple, it is thought cannot begin or end or change. Now essences are unchanging. Absolute beauty, for example, is always the same, whereas 'beautiful' things continuously change. Things seen are temporal but the things unseen are eternal. The body is seen but the soul is unseen, therefore, the soul is to be classified in the group of things that are eternal.

The School of Lurice

Upon the doctrine of metempsychosis was based the psychological system of the practical Cabala inaugurated by the Cabalist of the School of Lurice. According to them, all the souls destined for the human race were created together with various organs, of Adam. As there are superior and inferior organs so there are superior and inferior souls according to the organs with which they are respectively coupled. Thus, there are souls of the brain, of the eyes and of the head etc. Each human soul is a spark from Adam. The first sin of the first man caused confusion among various cases of souls so that even the purest soul received an admixture of evil. Thus, the state of confusion, which gives a centimal impulse, prevailed. Evil will cease with the arrival of the Messiah, who will establish the moral system in the world and new basis. Until that time, man's soul, because of deficiencies, cannot return to the source and has to wander not through the bodies of men but through inanimate things. If a man's good deeds overweigh his evil ones, his soul has to pass into a human body, otherwise into that of an animal. Incest causes the soul to pass into body of an unclean animal, adultery into that of an ass, pride in a leader of a community into that of a bee, forgery of amulets into that of a cat, cruelty towards the poor into that of a crow and so on and so forth for varying degrees of lapses computed for various types of inferior birth.

Note: *The above may be seen as a classic comparison of hell in our Purāṇas.*

Impregnation of Soul

A quite new development of the doctrine of metempsychosis was the theory of impregnation of souls propounded by the Cabalist of Luria School. According to this theory, a purified soul that has neglected some religious duties on earth must return to earthly life and unite with the soul of a living man in order to make good such neglect. Further, the soul of a man freed from sins appears again on earth to support a weak soul unequal to its task. Thus, for instance, those of Moses, conditioned, supported the soul of Samuel and this shows that three souls of homogeneous nature can occur at one time.

Note: *We have our examples of re-birth to cope up with the unfulfilled desires, overtaken by death.*

Schopenhauer

There is no such thing as happiness for an unfulfilled wish causes pain and attainment brings satiety. Instinct urges men to procreation, which brings into existence a new occasion for suffering and death. That is why shame is associated with the sexual act. Suicide is useless; the doctrine of transmigration, even if not literally true, conveys truth in the form of a myth.

Cathari [13th Century]

The tenets of the Cathari cannot be known with certainty, as we are entirely dependent on the testimony of their enemies but there is good deal that is almost beyond question. It seems that Cathari were dualists and that like the Gnostics, they considered the Old Testament of Jehovah a wicked demur, the true being only revealed in the New Testament. They regarded matter as essentially evil and believed that for the virtuous, there is no resurrection of the body. The wicked, however will suffer transmigration into the bodies of animals. On this ground they were vegetarian abstaining even from eggs, cheese and milk. They however ate fish because they believed that fishes are not sexually generated.

Aristotle

The doctrine of Aristotle leads easily to misunderstanding in his book "On the soul". He regards the soul as bound up with the body and ridicules the Pythagoras doctrine of transmigration. The soul seems to perish with the body. "It indubitably follows that the soul is inseparable from the body". But he adds, "At any rate certain parts of it such as the body and the soul are related as a matter form". "The soul must be a substance in the sense of the form of a material, body having life potentiality within it. But substance is actuality and thus soul is the actuality of the body as above characterized. Soul is the substance in the sense, which corresponds to the definitive formula of a thing's essence. That means that it is the essential whatness of a body of the character just assigned [having life]. The soul is the first grade of activity of a natural body having life potentially in it. The body is so described as a body, which is organized. To ask whether soul and body are one is meaningless as to ask whether the matter and shape given to it by the stamp are one and the same. Self-nutrition is the only psychic power by plants. The soul is the final cause of the body.

Plato's Cosmogony

The creator, Timacus says, made one soul for each star. Souls have sensation, love, fear and anger. If they overcome these, they live righteously, but if not, not. If a man lives well, he goes after death to live happily forever in the star. But if lived badly, he will in the next life be a woman, if he or she persists in evil doings, he or she will become brute and go on through transmigration until at last reason conquers. God puts some souls on earth, some on the moon, some on the other planets and stars and lift it to the gods to fashion their bodies.

The Cretans

The chronology of the Cretans history is derived from Egyptian objects found. Crete and Cretan objects found in

Egypt throughout our knowledge is dependent on archeological evidence. There is some evidence of belief, deeds on earth, receive reward or retribution. On the whole, Cretans were to have been cheerful people and opposed to gloomy superstitions. The bullfights were religious celebrations.

Mohammedan Culture

Auerroes was concerned to improve the Aristotle's arlic interpretation, unduly influenced by Neo Platonism gave a sort of relevance more than Auicenna to aristotle, the founder of the religion. He holds the view that the existence of God could be proved by the reasons independently of revelation, a view also held by Thomas Aquinas. As regards to immortality, he seems to have adhered closely to Aristotle, maintaining that the soul is not immortal but, your intellect is. This however, does not secure personal immortality since intellect is one and the same, when manifest in different persons. This view was naturally combated by Christian philosophers. Auerroes, like most of the Mohammedan philosophers, though a believer, was not a rigid orthodox. There was a sect of complete orthodox theologians, who objected to all philosophy as deleterious to faith. One of these named Algazel wrote a book called 'Destruction of philosophers' pointing out that since all necessary truth is in the Koran, there is no need for speculation, independent of revelation. Aurroes replied by a book called 'Destruction of the Destruction'. The religious dogma, the Algazel specially upheld against Philosophers were the creation of the world in time out of nothing, the reality of the divine attributed and the resurrection of the body. Auerroes regards religion as containing philosophic truth in allegorical form. This applies in particular to creation, which he, in his philosophic capacity, interprets in an Aristotelian fashion.

Heraclitus

The search for something permanent is one of the deepest instincts leading man to philosophy. It is derived, no doubt, from love of home and desire for a refuge from danger. We find accordingly that it is most passionate in those whose lives are most exposed to catastrophe. Religion seeks permanence in two forms – god and immortality. In God is no variableness, neither shadowed of turning the life after death is eternal and unchanging. The cheerfulness of nineteenth century turned the men against this static conception, and modern liberal theology believes that there is progress in heaven and evolution in godhead. But even in this conception there is something permanent, namely progress itself and its immanent goal. And a dose of disaster is likely to bring hope back to their older super-terrestrial forms, if life on earth is despaired of; it is only in heaven that peace can be sought.

Kant

"God, freedom and immortality are three ideas of reason". Pure reason leads to form these ideas. It cannot itself prove their reality. The moral law demands justice i.e. happiness proportional to virtues. Only providence can insure these and has evidently not insured it in this life. Therefore, there is a god and future life and there must be freedom since otherwise there would be no such thing as virtue.

Note: *The above five lines of Kant are far reaching concluding remarks on transmigration that meet all the hypothesis – the bricks and mortar to build the palace of re-birth, beautifully and elegantly. These are the assumptions of our second chapter to proceed with immortality, mentioned above pertains to the soul, the vedantins call Atma, which is eternal.*

CHAPTER II

Evolved Evolution

CHAPTER II

Evolved Evolution

Some enter a womb of a mother
That they enjoy in embodied state;
And others fuse into plants,
As knowledge and their deeds dictate.

—*Kaṭhopaniṣad-V-7*

Attached to this world, one who acts self seeking
Enjoys the result of his action later;
He wanders about because of his action,
Reborn with the gods, the fathers or elsewhere.

—*Śvetāśvatara Upaniṣad-V-7*

We have our conclusion based on the statements of the Scriptures and reasons, that the cause of the **transmigration** – that is the unending cycle of birth and death and sufferings relates to the universal law of cause and effect. Some use the terminology as the 'causation'; both are one and the same. We formulate the groups that are the cause of birth and rebirth and the groupings are:

- The actions [*Karma*] that had free will – that is to act on the specified base line or not to act or could be different way altogether? – general application of the law of transmigration.
- The desires and attachment of the individuals towards certain objects to own or to associate in some way or long

for it in the mind repeatedly which could not be secured during the life time. – Specific condition.

❖ A divine mission. The adjuncts acquired pertain to certain task of Lord, a link in the chain. The *devatas* [super humans] come down to be part of the play or to support the role of *avatāra puruṣa* remembering his role, as a king on the stage knows that he is not the king but an actor. The performance has neither reality nor any effect to which one can be held responsible by the *karma,* whereas a king of the relative world, when acts, the impact is felt in social, political and personal relation. This worldly king is also subjected to praise or censor by the law of causation like others to reap the fruits of his own merits/demerits, *sañcita* and *āgāmi karmas,* on the plan of the *karma* theory of transmigration into higher or lower world of enjoyment and sufferings.

One may ask as how to know who is subjected to the law of *karma* and who is the liberated one? The pure one knows well; if one does not know then he need not know. If someone is wealthy, that would not benefit others, one has to earn own wealth to enjoy it.

It is to be understood that the part of the action of life on the earth, which has not been imposed on, as result of actions done in the pervious existence, one is not liable to pay or gain anything. This action being independent of the previous action, one may perform as in a practical classroom to help those who deserve and desire.

Some examples of that kind may be apt here. Sri Ramakrishna Paramahamsa was *already* pure from birth and was a liberated soul as one may call him, *Jīvan mukta,* but even after that, he continued to live the life of common man serving the society. This part of his life is not going to add anything extra as there is nothing to add to the *Infinite*, which is already full and complete. The action is to be defined as service for the sake of service or life of blessedness. Another example is that of *gopas* of *dvāpara yuga*, who were part of the divine sports and chose to come down, so as to be in the company of the Lord Kṛṣṇā, the main character. These *gopas* were all liberated souls but became part of the game for its continuity or to say to move the wheels of the events in its logical direction, it was to go. All those were illumined ones and one should not take them as they appeared. The ignorant ones try to add common dimension to the divine sportsman.

Similarly, Sri Rāma incarnated in *treta yuga* to redeem his devotees and to teach the world an idealism – an ideal son, king, father, husband and master. In this play, there was need to open many knots to continue the stage play to be appealing to the common man. Sri Hanuman, who was a part of Lord Siva's glory, there was no need for any extra merit of devotion, sincerity and faithfulness to be brought into the life span but he associated with all these in which he was already well versed. He demonstrated out of his free will and compassion to serve the humanity in serving Sri Rāma in his mission that has to go in normal example of a devoted soul. Humans can learn from human beings only as that can only be understandable, being on the common ground of evolution of thought, speech and body language. As far as the form of a monkey is concerned, that matches very well with human beings in many ways. In fact, the human beings are the evolution of the monkey species only.

Why should not we call these characters as incarnation as the role they played was supersensuous and supernatural with detachment. No. It may not be appropriate. Incarnations possess the full-fledged play of divinity and independence. There again incarnations are self-supporting entities, causes and effects both are combined into a single point. In contrast these assistants offer their assistances to supplement the cause and are also found depending upon that fountainhead – the incarnated personality. In *Rāmāyaṇa* episodes Sri Hanuman is though part and parcel of the play but stands at distance, when compared with Sri Rāma. Therefore, it will be more appropriate to call such manifested forms by the name as the sparks of the fire in the sports of the incarnation. The spark possesses qualities of the heat and light but does not function in isolation of its own and it is not the total unto itself.

What happens when these addendam are not added in the functioning and goal of the divine incarnation? Can the objectives be accomplished without these? Certainly incarnation of the God is not dependent on these means, but the whole play becomes supernatural. The impact of supernatural entities does not last longer for the lack of compatibility and comparison of reasons. The majority does not believe in supernatural entities and that cannot be a lesson for human beings, the difference being in the adjuncts. Our identity is closer with the person with whom we are more intimate like mother and father due to our body relationship. People generally get lost in wife and children as their sufferings become one's own as it were. This is *saṁsāra* when identified with matter through *ahaṁkāra.* Here we are making our point on the multiplicity of sparks in fire, the substratum. The *Jīva* that follows *Īśvara* in His mission is not stained with *karma* as associated with *Īśvara*, if the ignorance [*maya*] does not make its home through it.

The causation

कर्मणो ह्यपि बोद्धव्यं बोद्धव्यं च विकर्मण: ।
अकर्मणश्च बोद्धव्यं गहना कर्मणो गति: ॥

"It is needful to discriminate action, to discriminate forbidden action, and to discriminate inaction; inscrutable is the way of karma". —*B.G.IV-17*

The day after night, then night and again another day is the series and cycle. Similarly, the beings from their [origin] unmanifstation to manifestation [in their mid-state] become unmanifest again at the end. Further, the duration of day and night too varies by hours, days and months. Thus, variation and varieties are the facts of the nature, the cosmos. The nature is lofty and the beauty all around it surpasses all imaginations. Wonderful mountains, snow-capped peaks, dancing rivers, gorgeous oceans, colorful birds, trees and fruits that bring out the taste on the tongue before even putting it into the mouth are all the gifts of nature. The water creatures like multitude varieties of fishes and marine creatures; animals in the forests, the shades, the colours and contours are all the poetry of the poet of poets. All these and more are the adorations of creation that strike the mind with an 'ah! With an irresistible sense, prayer and praise go to the Creator, the unseen, though present everywhere, and is also the wonder of wonders.

On the other side of the creation, we see inequality and disparity in the universe. Twin brothers, sisters or brother and sister born together, brought up in similar environmental conditions and parental care are marked for quite opposite in both mental health and wealth. Someone is born with silver spoon and the other with no spoon at all. One is born crippled whereas another becomes cripple afterwards. Some have healthy body throughout the passage of life, for some it is shortlived. One lives up to old age; the other dies at birth itself. Some exhibit extraordinary talent in arts/music at the tender age itself when for others at that age, it is Greek and Latin. One gets into spirituality by mere hearing roadside discourses whereas one does not reach to that maturity even after twenty years of practice. There are prodigy geniuses and there are dull-headed idiots and fools. One lives to live, the other lives for others. There are contrasts in livelihood, lifestyle, health, pleasures, participation, understanding, undertakings, success, failure and speech in every activity of life that goes in harnessing the resources, sustenance and surplus. How and who is responsible for these differences? Someone may jump into a conclusion with confidence that all these are plays of accident. Others may reiterate that all these are the acts of god, who is beyond the blue and enjoys. We are helpless and He is all-powerful, omniscient and all knowing one. Another in the assembly looks up and addresses with grace packed up with confidence. "Friends! In this creation, nothing is left to chance or accident". Attributing to accident is a wilful accident of ignorance.

Nothing happens as accident. It is possible that we may not know the reason or cause but for that we cannot push the issues to an accident or chance. When we see a child, we know that there must be parents to the child as the child cannot fall from sky on a rainy or on some sunny day. So, consequently, there must be parents, parents to the parents and so on and ultimately every cause leads to its cause, which will ultimately lead to the Absolute. In the exercise of an analysis, food is the cause of the beings, earth is the cause of food, water is the cause of earth, fire is the cause of water and again fire becomes the effect of air. Similarly, the effect: air belongs to the space: the cause. The space becomes the effect of the cause Īśvara [Brahman with *Māya*, the adjunct]. In this manner, cause and effect [product] relation ultimately leads to *Īśvara*, whatever be the point of starting this analysis on any plane and of any object. This is the reason that all *Vedāntic* works contain the topic or discussion on creation of the universe, which is an important link between individual, the world and the Lord *[Īśvara]*. Thus, the law of causation is the universal law of *karma* where the event can be both the cause and effect, barring the Absolute One.

Transmigration of *Jīva* presupposes two constituents, the matter and the Spirit – Consciousness. The six kinds of modifications, which is the nature of matter, are: to exist, to be born, to grow, to change, to decay and to perish. The body is the complex construction and constituent of the five elements, which are matter, therefore, body undergoes the six modifications. The Spirit is the life force, or to be more precise, it is the Consciousness, which is neither born nor dies. It neither comes into being nor ceases to be and does not undergo the six modifications. It is unborn, eternal, constant and ancient. It is not destroyed when the body goes to destruction. Body is the abode of the individual soul to experience pleasure and pain, earned through one's own previous actions.

Behind the gross body, there is the subtle one, which operates the physical body. It is the Consciousness and *Prāṇa.* Thus, *Prāṇa* only is manifest to work out the results of the actions of the previous birth. *Prāṇa* means vital energy or the life-sustaining power in us. Although *Prāṇa* is one, it takes five different names on account of the five different functions it performs. The word *Prāṇa* includes the five manifestations of the vital force. First that power which moves the lungs and draws the atmospheric air from outside into the system. This is also called *Prāṇa.* Second is that power which throws out of the system such things that are not wanted. It is called *Apāna.* Third, it takes the name of *samāna,* as performing digestive functions and carrying the extract of the food to every part of the body. It is known as *Udāna* when it is the cause of bringing down food from the mouth through the alimentary canal to the stomach, and also when it is the cause of the power of speech. The fifth one is that which works in every part of the nervous system from head to foot, through every canal, which keeps the shape of the body, preserves it from putrefaction, gives health and life to every cell and organ, known by the name *Vyāna.*

The above with the non-composite elements of the gross body and the impressions, tendencies and ideas which are accumulated with the individual in the lifetime makes his subtle body to remain intact, to be expressed in the next birth. It is possible that there is balance of impressions of other births, which could not be exhausted and they are given priority with the immediate past. The impressions which have fructified are called '*prārabdha*' which has to be exhausted in order i.e. *prārabdha, sañcita and āgāmi* respectively, though not necessary as one part may combine with other for compensatory effect of the module.

What is *Karma*? *Karma* is action, both physical and mental, individually or combined together. To mention the *karma* more distinctly, it is motion, attraction, gravitation and repulsion; in the universal sense – walking, hearing, seeing and thinking is the organism. Whenever the senses and sense organs come in to play its function, whether it is right or wrong in the gaze of the public or in private, *karma* takes place. These actions effect into reactions and produce the result in the manner the universal law is ordained for. The result of the *karma,* [cause], the action must be seen on two planes. One is that in which we appreciate through sense perception and the other is unseen, unknown and the matrix to derive the result is beyond the physical mental and the domain of inference. We shall discuss some illustrations. One has performed a fire ritual, the direct result or reaction is that some materials have been consumed by the fire. Brahmins were fed to their content and *dakṣiṇa* for partaking food and for officiating in the ritual was given, thus some money had been spent and changed hands. There were some words of praise and satisfaction on the mental plane of the individual who had performed as an achievement towards the noble and religious act and the beneficiaries had some elation and gratitude for having been honoured by the host.

But the result emerged at the divine or unknown plane, the merits and demerits, which bring pleasure and happiness, is not open to understanding in the absence of the knowledge of the conversion factor and constants. However, a broad classification can be inferred as good or when it hurts someone as bad or both. There is hardly any action *[karma]* in which all good or all bad possibilities are there. Majority or predominance has to be the yardstick for its classification:

- One that fulfills the general interest and common good of the society at large is considered as good.
- The *karma, which is performed with selfish motive at the cost of majority hardship or hurts someone, is bad.*
- *The one, which has balanced effects, are the mixed ones.* [A combination of common interest of the individual and the majority].

It may be taken note that the phrases used above as 'the general and common to the society' include all beings – men, animals, insects, environment of present, future, in wider sense of living and welfare that carry with it, homogeneous peace and tranquillity [at internal and external levels].

The law of cause and effect or the action and reaction is dovetailed into the transmigration of the *Jīva*, which is a philosophy as well as religion. The individual or the *Jīva* who is subjected to a large number of minute activities of the mind – substances of different names labelled as longings, tendencies, thoughts, ideas and impressions, every bit of these are combined together to form the action and reaction. Each individual personality and character is the grand total of the results of previous mental actions and is also the cause of the future changes in the character. In the train of cause and effect, each effect is latent in the cause and each cause is evidently present in the product. Every character is included in the cause as well as in the effect and this law of *karma* gets inculcated in the grand truth of nature. To illustrate, a seed contains the whole tree in potential form and produces the tree and the tree in turn produces seeds again. However, the tree and the seed do not reflect the actual plan of cause and effect as the tree does not commit to any action or able to reflect the pleasure and pain. So we cannot attribute any merits and demerits to the seed. It just proves the biological law that man begets man and tree begets a tree. Mango tree will bear mango fruit and coconut tree bears coconut. There cannot be things contrary to the phenomenon.

However, if the law is extended to the plan of *karma*, this is the answer to the citation submitted earlier as why there is disparity in character like good and bad or why one individual behaves this or that way, why one suffers and is miserable while the other enjoys life and is happy as in the context – the seed is previous deed and tree is the result, again new seed for future result. We have not to look for scapegoats to blame one lot, not even to Him, who dispenses the fruits of our action. He is always neutral and hates/loves no one and no one is to be punished or rewarded at His will. The pleasures and pain, happiness and sorrow are returns for everything that we possess in the life, is the product [effect] of our previous action or *karma*, both at physical and mental planes. The future course of the enjoyment and sufferings shall come from our present thoughts, acts and its activation. The hypothesis of predestination and grace are misplaced ideas and fall short under the doctrine of action – *karma*. It must be very clearly understood that the *Jīva* reaps the fruits of its previous acts and deeds of his own.

One who has faith in the law of *karma*, believes in its operation and effectiveness, is free from prejudices. He believes that he is creating his own destiny and thus careful in exercising his free will. He learns from experience and is more moral, performs virtuous acts and stands on a better rational ground like the one who abides by the traffic rules not because of the fear of constable [police] but for the common safety. He will not jump the signal even when there is no one to watch and regulate the traffic. He is aware of the fact that every wrong move will react upon himself some or the other time. Thus, one is blessed with a reaction-free life, an entitlement to happiness, peace, tranquillity and enlightenment born of self-understanding, not out of selfishness.

The two other components of the universal law of *karma* are the law of compensation and the law of retribution, which explain the varieties and types of nature, meaning that every cause must bear with similar effect or reaction. There is balance between the action and reaction so also in their nature. There is no loss or gain in their equation with each other and also they stand in perfect equilibrium and justice. Let us see in the following illustration how the nature presents equal and opposite reaction. Here is an interpolation of action and reaction, which may be the basis for apportionment of fruits for the actions together or vice versa in one plane or the other. The compensation may be made out from the meaning of *Karma and Karma yoga. Karma* glorifies the doer – the *Karta,* the agent who wants compensation for his specific actions and that may be in the terms of positive or negative results, again extending the *samsāra.* The incremental compensation of *Karma yoga* is purification of mind – *citta śhuddhii* that may shorten the *samsāra* being a forward move towards the means. For any value-added action, there is some advantage in the form of happy situation, such as health, wealth [worldly and divine], name and fame etc., and these are considered to be compensation in a desirable sense as they correspond to the good and noble action.

The diverse phase of nature is given the name 'retribution'. Retribution is the negative value or disadvantageous – the unethical code of conducts; say stealing or harming someone.

The immediate retribution is the corporal punishment through the laws of the land. If one manages to escape, then there is the divine justice and the retribution may be the punishment of suffering in *lokas* and *samsāra* etc. These are the plans of the creator and to meet these provisions, there are variations at various levels of plans and unfavourable conjunction in external and internal world – that is the present life and hereafter in the next birth.

A person who steals food starves in his next life. A liar becomes dumb in his next life. A stealer of oil is born as cockroach and stealer of green vegetable is born as a peacock. The stealer of salt gets only torn cloth to wear; likewise all offences get their punishment [retribution] as per the law of dispensation.

–G.Purāṇa

The compensations and retributions are the logical integration of the law of cause and effect. Mentioning any one, the other one gets expressed without expressing it distinctly.

Examples are:

- Mahatma Gandhi adored India and the Indians. The reaction and compensation is that the country now returns, worshipping him as the great and guiding star of India.
- Harder the application of strike on temple bell, louder is the rebound sound – reaction.
- Intense the earthquake, wider and deeper is the destruction – reaction.
- Melodious sound from the musical instrument is the compensation for the skill displayed in playing the instrument.

This law operates with same efficiency when we slip into the mental, intellectual, moral and spiritual phases. The very thought of Ganges creates mental harmony of purity, so is the case when we talk or think of temples, Gods and holy sages. In all these examples, the antecedent is the prime factor, the cause/background. We may face some difficulty in judging things properly, if the effect is not connected with their antecedents – the reason. Evil cause must give evil effect. A barren woman will not bear a child. None can skip the compensation and retribution process in this phenomenal world. The application with respect to affairs of events/actions in life, both at physical and mental level, evolving through tendencies are extremely intricate and also involve a cycle of beginning, growth and maturity [*prārabdha*]. The duration of cycle also depends on many other factors, spread over many births to reap the result i.e. compensation. It may be in the present life or after death, next or even next after. One has to stretch and extend without confining to the present birth only, as the beginning and end of this body, since our present is the result of the past. Future will see our present thoughts and deeds as the start of life, which is not similar to the lasting of the morning upto the start of next morning [24 hours duration disconnecting the previous and the future days]. We find at times very disappointing compensation of short duration, especially when we account for the many wet and gloomy unpleasant happenings on the same stand as the normal day. It is impossible to explain these fragments as the eternal life of *Jīva* consists of the chain of lives, not of 24 hours or hundred years. But one must be assured of perfect balance and justice, when the span of life is taken on proper denomination, which is neither known nor fixed to our own demand.

Now we come to explain to ourselves the retribution factor. It is a negative compensation so as to take it as a punishment, which extends not only to the present span of life but also to the next or next to next, same as the compensation. This retribution is the inexorable necessity in nature. First it operates in the inner nature of the embodied soul and thereafter it manifests into the external circumstances, in the shape of gain/loss, prosperity/adversity in health/disease etc. One is supposed to pay the right price/penalty through sufferings for our wrong doings but not for the standard/good deeds, virtuous living, wisdom and truthfulness as these proceed from God and they multiply into themselves for the benefit of the doer, its compensation. The crest of the laws, as they stand, is that the virtuous reward themselves and the sinners punish themselves for their mental and physical action, good or bad.

Pūrvamīmāmsakas and Buddhists do not place their confidence in personal gods [doctrine] but that the very system of the law on its own is capable of rewarding and punishing unto itself. *Pūrvamīmāmsakas* go a step further to the ritual or worship of the God without actually accepting the very existence of the god. Is it not surprising that when we say "*Indrāya svāhā*" and offer oblations without believing that there is god Indra behind? But they do believe in the efficacy of their action without any doubt. The doctrine of *karma* is the fundamental principle of the philosophy and religion of Hindus and others who have belief on the principle of transmigration. Inference is made that all reactions come back to the source from which it was generated or proceeded. Therefore the identity of the thinker, doer, enjoyer or sufferer is necessary. [Buddhists differ on this point.] As *karmas* are beginningless, therefore, the individual soul also must be beginningless.

The stored *karmas* are grouped into three groups and they are known as '*Sañcita, Prārabdha* and *Āgāmī*'. Those who believe in the noble doctrine of *karma* are not disturbed in the inequalities with respect to birth, fortune, intellect and capabilities that they have held them with pride. The very knowledge and understanding of universal truth hold men back from weary life of human being, blaming the Lord, who is the creator of beings. This law of *karma* and the individual together is made for each other. This law bestows freedom of action and thought, thus one is also free to mar or make oneself. This doctrine is capable of showing ray of hope for better future, better sense and better harvesting. It also directs one to live a moral, virtuous and spiritual life of today and bear the burden and sufferings that have befallen and be calm and composed.

Identification with Desire

The man with desires keeps brooding on them; because of desires, he has rebirths repeatedly. But to him, whose desires are fulfilled and who has realized the *Ātman*, all desires vanish, even here on earth. *–Muṇḍakopaniṣad III-2-2*

When one is with unfulfilled desires at the time of death, he is identified with it. This identification prefixes objects of senses and an attachment suffixes anger delusion, confused memory and ruin of reason as its cause and effect respectively in the series. What is desired, it resolves, what is resolved it works out and what it works out it attains. The mind, on seeing something to be attained, forms the false notion that it has to get that one. Setting its heart on that, it becomes identified with the desires further. If the desire is frustrated, it takes the form of anger and that follows the chain. Muṇḍakopaniṣad says: "He who longs for objects of desire, making much of them, is born along with those desires in places where he will realize them". All that we do mentally and physically, create wave like effects in our mind and stay there as our *samskāra or vāsana* – impressions. This *vāsana* or longing for worldly pleasures and objects remains latent for hundreds of births. The only way to get over this is the satisfaction of the enjoyment of them. This very *vāsana* is the manufacturer of the gross body in the womb. Parents afford suitable environment to channel through, but the real agency that works behind for selection of the environment and development is the *vāsana* that has gone with the subtle body after death in contracted form. Therefore, the self happens to identify with the desires alone. Its identification with other things, though may be present, is subordinate to this desire. Hence, having identification with the desire alone, it resolves to achieve.

Regarding desire, there is this pithy verse: "When all the desires that dwell in the heart [mind] are gone, then he, having mortal, becomes immortal and attains Brahman in the very body. Just as the lifeless slough of snake is cast off and lies in the anthill, so lies this body. Then the self becomes disembodied and immortal, the *prāna*, the light, the Brahman". But when the body with awareness constituted mainly of desires, life impulses that drove the life movement are still active. And till all these desires, these impressions remain, the soul, cannot go forward to its place of rest – peace and tranquillity.

If the person had led a good life, while on earth, a life turned bright, harmonious and love, these things remain after death in the form of much idealized awareness. There is great beauty, great joy, and great felicity all around. This is what is called heaven. Similarly, a person, who has led an evil life, a life of gloom, violence, betrayal etc., finds himself in the aura of *asura or Yamaloka*, the dark world. And all the evils and dark conditions and actions are present in an exaggerated form and the person suffers. He has to work out all of them – the hell. It is in this sense one carries one's hell and heaven unto himself. This may not be taken as poetry. It is a fact. It is we who have to decide what we have to have after death. Things do not end by leaving the physical body, such as suicide. There is the law governing evolution, the soul that has crossed the animal belt and progressed into the human body need not normally go back and occupy an animal body. All that happens is that the *prāṇamaya śarīra,* the desirous body descends and satisfies itself through animal like instruments of enjoyment. The conditions of hell and heaven are the storehouse of unfulfilled desires, constitute the vital body to work out and exhaust, which means that the being has to remain in *Prāṇamaya loka.* There, at that stage, maybe very low types of desires remain unfulfilled, which have to be fulfilled in very subtle way, in the subtle world. For example, the greed for food – the part of the subtle body which is filled with greed, determines to come down to earth, attach itself to someone or some creature and gets the desires satisfied, may be even through the form of a pig, known to be glutton. Similarly, the desire for sex through a subtle body of a goat or pig gets satisfied. The actual meaning of hell and heaven and being thrown into an animal body etc.

do not exist in the sense it is mentioned but it is the condition that prevails, where we go. There is nobody to punish us for the sins but ourselves through reaction – the cause rebound. Our fate is the child of past energies. The being in *prāṇamaya loka* has to exhaust its desires, exhaust what is held back. It is to help the beings at this stage that the *śrāddha* ceremonies are performed.

Our scriptures validate that when the ceremonies are done with proper understanding of the significance, when prayers are offered with thoughts and feelings of love and support, are directed to the departed soul, they reach and help the being to disentangle itself and become free from delusion in the *prāṇamaya loka.* Freed from the *prāṇamaya,* the soul moves to *manomaya,* the world of mind, for working out its mental prejudices, dogma and notions it held so tightly. When this also is accomplished, goes to the abode of rest to assimilate the experiences. After exhausting all these, the soul calls back its decision, that was made at the time of leaving the body and starts preparing similar body to accommodate the ideas, that actuated the decision for the specific experience desired by it.

The development of the sense organs that have been influenced must correspond to the principal desire, that is strongest and this is how the desires are expressed through the medium and form.

To illustrate:
The Lord says in the Gita:

पार्थ नैवेह नामुत्र विनाशस्तस्य विद्यते ।
न हि कल्याणकृत्कश्चिद्दुर्गतिं तात गच्छति ॥

"O Partha, neither in this world nor in the next is there destruction for him; for, the doer of good, O my son, never comes to grief". *–B.G.VI.40*

This also makes the point of continuity and involved evolution.

A *sadhaka* who slips from yoga will never fall into an inferior state than what he has already attained. He takes birth again on earth in the house of pure and prosperous to continue as a seeker with the requirements befitting to the attainment of the goal. According to law of *karma* souls take rebirth in the environment befitting their attainment. The one who transmigrates together with the work, that he did with attachment to its result, attains that result to which his subtle body or mind is firmly attached, i.e. for which he yearns, since he did the work out of a desire for that. The mind is called the subtle body, *Liṅga* śarīra, because it is the principal part of the faculties; the word *liṅga* means a symbol that which indicates the self. Therefore, only on account of this attachment in his mind, he attains the result through that action. This proves that desire is the root of transmigratory existence. Exhausting the results of work, whatever he did in his life, after experiencing them, he returns from that world to this world for work since work holds foremost place in this world. After working again, he, on account of attachment to the results, again goes to the next world and so on. Thus does the man, who desires, transmigrate. Therefore, the man who does not desire does not transmigrate anywhere. A knower of Brahman, who has routed out his desires, may work, but it will produce no baneful results.

The doctrine of *karma* and rebirth forms an important part of *upaniṣadic* teachings and has exerted greatest influence upon Hindu society. It is one of the strong pillars on which Hindu *dharma* rests. This is the answer to the question 'what becomes after death of a man?' This also explains the inequalities between man and man at the time of birth and also the basic brick of the moral foundation of the universe in which virtue is rewarded and vices harassed. This cannot be applied to the soul or the *Ātma*, which is beyond the birth and death, unaffected by the time, space, thus beyond the law of causation. It has reference to the *Jīva* or the embodied soul only. At the time of death, action of the man remains in the seed form and the seed develops when one assumes new body on the earth or any other plane of manifestation. "Every man born on the earth is fashioned by himself. Man is altogether and throughout composed of desires '*kāma*' and proportionate to his desire, so is his discretion '*kratu*' , in proportion to his discretion, so he performs acts – '*karma*' , in proportion to his acts, so does it result to him".

The migrating substance being fixed in quantity and quality, the embodied soul chooses to form according to its taste, desires and bent of character.

Some Illustrations

1. Our Purāṇa personifies the principle and the desire dovetailed to the law of *karma*. Pūtanā was a demoness who was killed by Kṛṣṇa at Ambādi. She was the daughter of a demoness called Kaitavī and was the maid-servant of the wife of Kaṁsa. Pūtanā, in her previous birth, was born as the daughter of Mahābali, bearing the name of Ratnamālā. When

Vāmana appeared before Mahābali during the time of latter's *Yajña,* Ratnamālā mentally desired thus: "Oh if only this Vāmana became my child! I could have then breastfed him." Vāmana, the Omniscient, understood the desire of Ratnamālā. So, during the incarnation of Kṛṣṇa, Ratnamālā was born as Pūtanā and Kṛṣṇa gave her salvation by drinking her breast-milk and squeezed her to death.

—BrV Purāṇa, chapter 4-10

Here we find two-prong unfolding of the universal law:

- The fulfilment of desire to give breast-feed, to be suckled by the Lord.
- The intention of killing and getting killed.

2. Purāṇa depicts the story of Bharata to show how attachment leads to rebirth. Bharata was the eldest son of king Ṛṣabha. Bharata like his forefather was very erudite and affectionate and always respected his duties. He always meditated on the *Parmapuruṣa* in the form of Vāsudeva. He ruled the country for long and divided his kingdom among his sons and went to the *āśrama* of Pulaha Maharṣī to spend the rest of his life. Bharata lived there oblivious of the external world. He led a purely ascetic life. One day a thirsty pregnant deer went to drink water in a nearby pond. As it was drinking, it heard the loud roar of a lion. Frightened, the deer ran for its life and on the way delivered a child and the baby deer fell into the river.

Bharata happened to see the newborn deer floating on the river and took it to his *āśrama.* From then onwards, Bharata's mind was diverted from the spiritual to the mundane effort of taking care of the young deer. The deer followed him wherever he went and if it did no turn up after grazing,

Bharta went about searching for it weeping. Years went by. Bharta became old and died with the thought of the deer only. Because he died with the thought of the deer in his mind, he was reborn as a deer. The deer was aware of its previous birth and regretted that he spent the life of a human for the sake of a deer. The deer, therefore, left the house of its mother and went to the *āśrama* of Pulaha. The pious animal bathed daily in the river and died on the bank of the river. In its next life, the deer was born as the son of a Brahmin in the line of Aṅgiras. He was the only son of the Brahmin's second wife and the first wife had nine sons. In due course, the Brahmin died and the second wife jumped into the funeral pyre. As an orphan, Bharata was ill treated by his brothers and was asked to look after the cattle. With great forbearance, Bharata did all what he was told to do. One day midnight when Bharata was keeping watch over the fields of his brothers, *Caṇḍālas* were making merry over the birth of a child. When they were bringing a man for offering to the goddess, he escaped. While searching for a substitute, they came across Bharata, bound him with ropes and took him for offering to the goddess. The effulgence of the Brahmin astounded Kāli and getting angry for bringing such a pious Brahmin for *bali,* the goddess devoured the *Caṇḍalas* and allowed the Brahmin to go free. Escaping from there, Bharata reached a village. The king of that place known as Rahūgaṇa was going to see sage Kapila and the Brahmin was asked to be one of the palanquin-bearers. As they were moving, the palanquin was shaking because of wrong steps. The king reprimanded Bharata. Bharata gave the king befitting replies based on the ethics of *Vedānta.* The erudition of Bharata greatly impressed the king; he stepped down and asked him to accept him as a disciple. Then onwards Bharata went for meditation and attained liberation. —*Bh.P 5th Skanda*

3. Śivaśarman, a well versed Brahmin, had five sons, who were all devoted to their father. The father decided to test the devotion of each of the sons. By the blessings of Lord Śiva, he had all the *siddhis* and illusion power. He tested his first four sons by ordering each one of them to difficult tasks and the sons obeyed their father, including offering their head. The father was pleased with the four sons and blessed them. Now he wanted to test his fifth son named Śomaśarman. He told his son that he wanted to go for a pilgrimage and asked to keep the pot containing nectar, which was brought by the fourth son. The son kept it very carefully for ten years. Now Śivaśarman returned from his pilgrimage. By magic, he had become a leper and made his wife also a leper. Śomaśarman felt pain to see his parents in this condition and served them meticulously. He foresaw their desires and necessities and satisfied them. Yet, the father used to lose his temper and beat him but the son did not lose his temper at any time.

Time passed on thus. The parents were pleased with their son but wanted to give one more test. After stealing away the nectar in the pot by magic, he asked the son for the pot of nectar. When Śomaśarman looked into the pot, to his horror, it was missing. But he took the pot to his father saying to himself, "Let there be nectar, if I have served my elders well and if I am truthful and observed pure austerity". The pot was filled with nectar. Śivaśarman blessed his son and by his power of his yoga ascended to *Vaikuṇṭha* along with his wife. After this Śomaśarman began practising the most intense form of *tapas*. When the time of his death was near, *asuras* approached him. Fear of *asuras* gripped him while he was in deep meditation. As he breathed his last thinking about the *asuras*, he was born as Prahlāda in his next life, son of Hirṇyakaśipu. Prahlāda had the fortune of seeing Lord Viṣṇu before him; the Lord told him that as he had a desire to be a king in his previous birth, he had to be born as a king.

—PP-Bhumikhaṇḍa

CHAPTER III

Obscure Oblations

CHAPTER III

Obscure Oblations

अन्नाद्भवन्ति भूतानि पर्जन्यादन्नसम्भवः ।
यज्ञाद्भवति पर्जन्यो यज्ञःकर्मसमुद्भवः ॥

कर्म ब्रह्मोद्भवं विद्धि ब्रह्माक्षरसमुद्भवम् ।
तस्मात् सर्वगतं ब्रह्म नित्यं यज्ञे प्रतिष्ठितम ॥

"From food beings become; from rain is food produced; from *Yajña* rain proceeds; *Yajña* is born of *karma*".

"Know *karma* to have risen from the Veda and the Veda from the imperishable. The All-pervading Veda is, therefore, ever centred in Yajña." —*B.G.III-14 & 15*

Matter and Spirit

Rebirth is possible only for those who were born before. The world of Philosophers, scientists and the seekers of Truth are unable to lay their hands on that, which is supposed to have been born is – the Spirit or Matter? When we talk of rebirth, confusion is confounded. The theory of Conservation of energy pegs us to the fact that no new thing comes into being at all; it is only the modification of the matter that takes place, conditioned by space and time. 'Born' means a new thing, which did not exist before. Now coming to the physical body of an individual, it was already in the elementary form.

Well! When we said that matter is not born, then perhaps is it the Spirit? It is also not possible. The matter undergoes at least modification, whereas as far as Spirit is concerned, there cannot be even that. The Spirit is eternal, unchangeable, all pervading and infinite. Perhaps now the question is then what is that birth we mean here? We see a child coming into existence; grow to maturity, old age and disappearing suddenly. What do we call these phenomena, if we do not want to give the name 'birth'?

Precisely it is a union of the matter and Spirit. To give a generic name to this, one has to understand about Consciousness or Awareness, which is nothing but Spirit. It is present always, at all places and at all times. During the birth of an individual, the Spirit is manifest. Here the word 'birth' is used to convey the idea, which is familiar and commonly known. In the real sense, nothing is born, but it is only manifestation. Even at the time of deluge [*Pralaya*], nothing is lost as everything returns from its gross state to subtle state and again at the dawn of the creation, dormant things come into manifestation.

To accept the word 'dormant', we have to go to the sequence and consequence of seed and tree. The whole tree including the leaves, fruits, flowers and even the future seeds are in dormant condition in that one seed, that becomes a huge tree at appropriate condition of the time and space. The seed is the cause and the tree with its attributes is the effect. Again the tree becomes the cause for the seed and thus this world too goes on and on in a cyclic order, the cause and effect relationship goes on perpetuating. In a cycle, the first beginning of the cycle cannot be traced and breaking our head over it, is neither going to solve nor lighten our problems in any way, as any point on the periphery of the cycle constantly is preceding and succeeding again and again.

Micro and Macro

Like many constituents of the universe, whole and part or total and individual principle is applicable to our subtle and causal bodies, which are all matter in nature. An individual has seeing, hearing, lifting and walking power or energy at micro level and there is the total of all the powers, put together, known as the substratum [*adhiṣtānam*] and this is identified with the *adhiṣtāna devata*, who presides over the total functional energy. This power or energy is lent to the individual faculty and so long these are available, one can function through these. As soon as these are withdrawn, one cannot function, that is, the particular faculty does not respond, in spite of the organs being very much there, known as *golakam* i.e. though the eyes are there but one cannot see, ears are there but unable to hear, hands and legs are there but without its capacity to function thereto.

Therefore, it can be seen that for each function, we have the corresponding presiding deity. For the power of the eyes, it is the Sun god [the power and not the solar disc], for the mind, it is moon, for the power of legs, it is *Viṣṇu,* for the lifting power, it is *Indra devata,* for the hearing power, it is the Lord of the quarters, for the breathing power, it is *Vāyu devata,* for evacuation, it is Yama and for procreation, it is *Prajāpati* and so on. All the powers put together, it is *Hiraṇyagarbha*, who is the sum total of all the powers to whom the individual power [*the devata*] is subordinate. In modern example, we may compare it to the minister and the

Prime Minister. Similarly, the total of the gross bodies is known by the name *Virāt* and the total of the causal bodies is the *Īśvara. Īśvara* with adjuncts [*māya*] functions as the Omnipresent, Omniscient, the very Creator and sustainer, unto whom all resolve during *Pralaya* and remain in unmanifest state of existence. He brings forth the creation i.e. manifestation to exhaust the fruits of the past actions of the individuals and total actions of the cycle. Our physical body – the *annamaya kośa* consisting of the flesh, bone, bone marrow, blood and skin – all of them are inert in nature, made of the five great subtle elements grossified. The five great subtle elements, namely the sky, air, fire, water and earth too are inert in nature but inherited the quality of *satva, rajas and tamas* from the *māya – the mother*, whose projections they are. The other properties of the elements are sound for the sky, sound and touch for the air, sound, touch and form for the fire, sound, touch, form and taste for the water and the earth has got apart from all the above four qualities, it has its own quality of smell. Subtler the element, lesser the attributes and grosser the element, more are the number of attributes. Successive elements inherit the qualities of the elements from which it has appeared apart from its own quality. For example, air has appeared from sky and so it has the quality of sky – the sound apart from its own quality of touch. Causal body is the cause of the subtle and gross body and similarly the causal state is the cause for the dream and waking state. The above distinctions are between the state of existence and the formation of the bodies; however, all of them are inert in nature.

Kindling the Essence

The earth is the life and essence of all the bodies – moving and non-moving – a honey to all beings, water is the essence of earth being pervaded. Herb is the effect of water and water is the cause. Flowers of herbs, fruits of flowers, man of truth and the seed of man for another, that emanates from all parts of the body are respective essence. The seed finds its abode in the woman where the birth is through the womb and on the same principle, but through different instrumentation are the births for other base. The agencies of propagations are:

Womb	Human and animal world.
Egg shell	Birds and reptiles.
Moisture	Insects and microbes.
Break open	As in the case of plants and trees.

The Fire Rituals [Sacrifices]

The *Agni-hotra* [fire sacrifices] is a *karma* coined by *Vedic wisdom* – a grand design demonstrating action [*karma*] and effect [reaction and its product]. The Veda calls it by another name *Yajña.* All *Yajñas* stand for the *karma* in the glory of the Lord.

ब्रह्मार्पणं ब्रह्म हविर्ब्रह्माग्नौ ब्रह्मणा हुतम ।
ब्रह्मैव तेन गन्तव्यं ब्रह्मकर्मसमाधिना ॥

—BG.IV-24

The nature of *Yajña* – the oblation is Brahman, that which is offered in the fire – the clarified butter is Brahman, the material content of the oblation is Brahman, the fire is

Brahman, the receiver of the oblation is Brahman, the *yajamana* – the one who is engaged in the *yajña* is Brahman and the very action through which the *Yajña* is performed is also Brahman.

Thus, there is non-duality in the apparent *triputi,* the doer, the action and the desire [*karta*, *kāryam* and *kāma*]. The varieties and types, what we have talked before under 'compensation and retribution', may be aptly visualized for fullest comparison through the examples here.

- The performance of sacrifice is for Devas alone. Others offer self as sacrifice by the self, verily in the fire of Brahman.
- Some others offer the hearing and other senses in the fire of restraint, while others offer sound and other sense objects as sacrifice in the fire of senses.
- Offerings of all the actions of senses and functions of the life energy as a sacrifice in the fire of the self-control, kindled by knowledge.
- Yet there are offerings of wealth, austerity and *Yoga* as sacrifice, added to other sacrifices, such as self-denial, extreme vows, sacred study and knowledge.
- Inclusion in the list of sacrifices are outgoing breath in the incoming breath and the other way, the incoming breath into outgoing breath, which means the regulation and control of the food and food habits.

There are some examples of holistic views that in every event of the function of the nature there are these things that form and confirm to the subject, object, instrument of the action, the doer and the benefits of the action.

The basic *Vedic* infrastructures of the rituals are:

1. The doer of the sacrifice – *karta.*
2. The action – the performance of the ritual that is enjoined by the Vedas in the fire. [*Karma-kāṇda*]
3. The benefits [results], the very objective behind the performance, that is the desire which instituted the action.
4. Materials that are required in the performance. The collection of the materials and the implements employed, which form the oblations, come under this [Solid, semi-liquid and liquid]. Apart from these, it is also human and monetary resources. The *Vedic mantras* and the scriptural contents are known by the name *Daivi vittam* [divine wealth].

Transportation

In this highly imaginary context, we visualize the sacrificial fire and its various components, sparks, smoke and flame, etc. along with the oblations, which are offered in the ritual fire, the receiver and transfer to other gods, if the oblations are meant for others, than fire god himself. The oblation offered gets converted into the desired object [like currency exchange] and here is an example:

A man who is born has to die after exhausting his *Prārabdha karma.* The water is the rest of the body. When a person is dying, his speech merges into the mind, the mind merges into the *Prāṇa, the Prāṇa* into the fire and then fire merges into the Supreme deity. First, his speech fails but mind is still active, later mind ceases to function but he is still breathing, breath ceases but the warmth of the body remains [when the person is not yet dead] and when the heat goes away, everything is over. The fire is the fire, maintained by him during his lifetime, so is the fuel, the smoke, the flame, the cinder, the sparks, etc. and the oblation is the body in the last rite.

The Last Rite – The Oblation of The Body

When the body has become lifeless, it is taken to be consigned to the fire, the last ritual of the gross body. The very fire is known by the scriptural name *dakṣināgni.* The *Gārhapatya agni* that was tendered throughout the life after marriage, gave the right to such rites. Here the individual, who had offered oblations of different materials into the ritual fire *āhavanīyāgni*, now cannot offer anything any more but his own body. The people offer his body into the fire on his behalf. The *agni devata*, the fire god, having accepted it through the ritual gives in exchange another body that is capable of fulfilling the requirement of *bhoga* and *loka.* This subtle physical body is taken by the respective god for offering as oblation that is discussed under the caption of '*five oblations*', to return to human life, provided one is eligible for the next birth also in human form.

The Twin Paths of Travel

The *Jīvātma* transmigrating through death adopts either of the two paths, known by the technical name *Devayāna* or *Pitṛyāna* [the path of light or smoke – knowledge or ignorance] the one that leads to higher region and the other one lingering and lagging behind. This progression and regression is not due to astral light of days, months and years but the two paths are the allegorical expression of the path of merits and demerits that have been earned by the embodied soul, through the sojourn. [Living in particular abode – body]. It is the brilliance/progress or the ignorance or the stagnation and deterioration that are indicated through death. The path of light admits the clarity of awareness or the expansion of Consciousness while leaving the body, compared to the bright half of the moon and the six months of northern path of the sun, contrary to its darkness of the self-ignorance in the other, enshrouded as compared herein. Succeeding to the path of light is desirable, rather it should be a goal to gain the freedom from the cycle of birth and death which is to be attained, some time or the other, the earlier the better. The advantage of attaining the light path is the progressive goal of human birth. Knowing these two paths, the *yogi* is not deluded, which means one makes positive effort to act in such a manner by the proper performance of the rituals etc that is conducive, avoiding those which are not desirable.

The paths are also known as *Śukla and Kṛṣṇa gati. Śukla* stands for the bright path and *Kṛṣṇa* for the dark one. The dark can be understood as the one bereft of the light of knowledge or the ignorance as well. According to our scriptures, the paths are apart from each other and the life breath goes out of different orifice of the body. The traveller of the bright path emerges from the *suṣumna nādi* at the point in the middle of the head, known as *Brahmarandham.* To travel on the dark path, the breath comes out or leaves the body from other orifices, such as mouth, nose or eyes, etc.

Track Designated

Having practised austerity with faith – they travel, after death to the world of light. From the world of light, they go to the world of day; from the world of day to the world of bright fortnight; from the world of bright fortnight to the six months when the sun moves northward; from there they go to the year; from the year to the sun; from the sun to the moon; from the moon to lightning. The above description is of respective functional *devatas* to accept and guide. That someone, not human, receives them and leads to *Brahmaloka.* From *Brahmaloka*, one gets *kramamukti* – the path of gods.

The second path is for the person performing acts of social services and charity etc. and he goes through the path of smoke [*kṛṣṇa gati*], to the world of night; from the world of night they go to the world of dark fortnight; and from the world of dark fortnight they go to the world of six months when the sun moves to the south. That is not the world of year but the world of ancestors and from there they go to sky. From sky they go to the moon, the king *soma*, the food of the gods. Here the food means they are used for the services of the gods and not that they are eaten. Living in the world of moon to exhaust the fruits of the services rendered by them to the society, they go back to the society, the way came to the world of sky – air – smoke [mist] – cloud – rains – foodgrain [paddy, plants, beans and so forth], to become a *Puruṣa bīja* if eaten by the appropriate being to produce children exactly like themselves, thus good and bad births occur according to the deeds, like *Brahmaṇa*, *Kṣhatriya*, lower human beings or animals.

Those who do not go by either of these two paths described above, are born as small animals, insects etc. again and again and they are shortlived. Here the path means the ruler or the presiding deity of the light, dark, sky, day and year etc. as the guide to the destination so discussed. Light and dark also can be understood as happy journey and painful/difficult journey and so on. Normally, we experience comfort and discomfort when we go in I class of A.C. compartment, that can be compared to the general unreserved compartment, where there would not be sufficient space even to stand, smell, push and pull and so on. Bright and dark paths can be again understood in the terms of knowledge and ignorance and the resultant effect on the sense equipment at our disposal. Human beings have five sense organs, whereas in the case of lower beings, they have 4, 3 or 2 and so on, so is the enjoyment they get from them.

From One Body to The Next – The Death

The *Jīva* is likened to the travels from dream to waking state and back to dream and so on, till it attains that state from which there is no more travel involved. After all there must be some purpose or the cause for this back and forth journey and we have taken up these points for discussion in some other pages. Here the comparison is drawn to highlight the hardship one suffers when vacating the house presently occupied in order to occupy another one for rent. [Tenement] with lot of household luggage i.e., the karma earned.

In *Gīta* chapter 15 – 8, there is a reference "when the master [soul] acquires a body and when he leaves, he takes these and leaves like a breeze that carries the scents from their sources".

Why shifting of the house? There could be a number of reasons as we see, the reasons for death but some of them may be summarized as:

- The very purpose for which the body was adopted is over, that is fulfilment of the mission.
- The body has become weak and unworthy for further use due to depletion of the strength, due to modification – *vikāras.*
- Further experience of *prārabdha* is not possible through the existing type of abode [the body].

On death, the gross body is detached from the subtle body as its limiting adjuncts, goes making noises – the death rattle that causes, when breathing becomes difficult, which has been compared to a heavily loaded cart, goes on rumbling as the articles on the cart shake, making noises. The changes are in the body and the body parts, which were blessed by the individual or a particular *devata* and these *devatas* are blessed by the total. The presiding deity of the eyes – the sun grants the power of seeing, directed by the experiencer's past work, goes on helping in the functions of the eyes as long as he lives but ceases to help the eyes and is merged in his own self – the sun, when the man is about to die. He does not see, smell, taste, speak, hear, think and touch as these faculties have united with their respective presiding deities, who in turn cease to bless the organs of the dying one. These functional subtle bodies bid farewell and make themselves prepared to welcome again in the next body to the requirement and purpose.

How does the life force depart? It departs from the heart top and follows the channel of eyes or head or any other

part of the body along with vital force with the particular consciousness, that is the knowledge of work and past experiences. For example, when the past experience is related to knowledge, the Sun is the presiding deity of the eyes and symbol of knowledge. Similarly, other orifices of the body in question highlight the experiences as reasoned above – the subtle organs stand united within the heart. The self-effulgent intelligence of the Ātman is particularly manifest in the subtle body. A man attains that very object about which he thinks at the moment of death. There are number of scriptural supports to the idea very widely. At this point, everyone has a consciousness containing the imprints in the shape of the modifications of the mind with respect to the coming life – the very past work that goes to build the next body. Choosing of the thoughts at that particular moment of death is not possible as one is not independent to that extent, when one is not established in yoga and right knowledge. The law that operates is "one indeed becomes good through good work and evil through evil work". Since vocal organ of the dying man is united in fire, the nose in air, the eye in the sun, the mind in the moon, the ears in the quarters, the body in the earth, the heart's space in space, the hair in the body in herbs, that on the head in trees and the blood and seed in the water, where is then the man and his action? Therefore only the accumulated actions are solely responsible for the fresh action. Here we intend to discuss two more important points.

Whether the travel involved is later movement from one to another medium other than its own or is it uprooted completely from the point, simply landing on the other like a bird?

This is described as the movement of a leach that retains its grip on the existing straw, goes to the end of that, makes hold on another and when the grip is established, passes out itself through contraction on the first. The same way here also the next body becomes conscious, when the previous body becomes consciousless. In fact, the preparation of the next body starts immediately when in the first body. All thoughts and actions, both mental and physical, go on to build the next body simultaneously. However, there are free wills upto the last moment, which is lost with the last breath as in dream the Self creates a new body and dwells as it were in that dream body. That is how the formation and movement of the next body takes place. Body is the means of body, that is to say that the Self uses the present body to make further body and this goes on in succession. The idea behind is for better tomorrow but the good and bad works impede, especially the undesirable ones that throw back the progress.

The Five Oblations

Here we are talking about the return of the man who is neither liberated in the present birth nor has gone to *Brahma loka*, for liberation in due course and also those who slid down to lower world of existence.

This universe was but water [liquid oblation], connected with sacrifices in the beginning. The water produced *Satya* and *Satya* is Brahman. Brahman produced Prajapati and Prajapati in turn produced the gods. Human beings too have major portion as water. Thus, the first oblation that gives the subtle human body is also in the form of water. [*jala śarira*].

In the very morning, he should purify the clarified butter according to the mode of *sthālipāka* and offer *sthālipāka* oblation again and again, saying *svāhā* to fire, *svāhā* to animate, *svāhā* to the radiant sun, who produces infallible results. After offering, he takes up the remnant of the cooked food, eats part of it and gives the rest to his wife. Then washes the hands, fills the water vessel and sprinkles three times with the water on his wife saying "get up from here, Viśvavasu and find out another young woman [who is] with her husband" [to be uttered once only]. The husband then embraces his wife saying 'I am the vital force and you are the speech, you are speech, I am the vital force. I am *Sāma* and you are *Ṛg*. I am heaven and you are the earth, come, let us strive together so that we may have a male child'.

The fifth oblation is offered in the fire, the woman in sacrifice by the gods, the result is the birth of the man. The liquid water designates as faith, successively offered in the fire of heaven, rain god, this world, the man and the woman in the increasingly grosser forms, faith, moon, rain, food and seed respectively brings out what is called the man. The gross man has come out from the subtle water body given by the fire in exchange of the lifeless body offered to the fire as an oblation. And this subtle body undergoes modification through five fire oblations as discussed above. The knowledge and meditation on the five fires is to give the benefit of attaining northern path travel.

Five Fires

The heaven, the rain god, this world, man and woman.

Five Fuels

The sun, the year, the earth, the mouth [open] and *āśrama dharma*.

Five Oblations

The faith, the king moon, the rain, the food and the human seed.

Now let us see what discomfort is there on the fifth oblation, though it is not specific to this particular oblation but can be expressed more authentically compared to the points of other four oblations, under this title, the sufferings of the *Jīvas* in the womb, that is the association with the growth in the womb. By the force of previous *karma*, which is under the direction of the deity, the *Jīva* conveyed by the seed of the man enters into the womb so that his gross body may progress. In the course of a night, the mingling of the seed and the blood takes place, in five nights, it becomes a round semi-solid mass, in ten days, it becomes as hard as an apple or it may become a ball of flesh or an egg. In a month, the head is formed and in two months, the body is formed with hands, feet and other organs. By the end of three months, formation of nails, hair, bone and skin as well as penis and anus occur.

At the end of fourth month, the seven *dhatus* or forms of matter become differentiated. At the fifth month, hunger and thirst makes its appearance, at the end of six months, it is covered with external skin called *jarāyu* and in the right side of the abdomen, it begins to turn – to be in the state of motion. In the seventh month, it becomes possessed with

Consciousness and starts recollecting all the past lives and deeds in this land [*karma bhūmī*]. It perceives that its bondage is caused by the will of the Lord Hari. It prays **"I bow to the Lord, who remains in the same way, unassociated by conditions and unchanged and who shines with uninterrupted wisdom and whom I have realized in my afflicted heart. I who lie concealed, unreal as it may be, in the body composed of the five sheaths and who am the intelligent image reflected false as may be in the *'indriyas'*, the *guṇas* and the objects – I praise and bow to that Omniscient person [Lord] now in my view of glory unaffected by the condition, being the ruler of *prakṛti and Puruṣa*".** This creature grows feeding on the food, drinks, etc. consumed by the mother and remains in the disagreeable [horrible] hollows filled with urine and excreta from which creatures are born. On account of its softness, its body constantly is bitten by hungry worms, which are in the same hollow and is in great affliction and pain, it swoons every moment. Touched by the bitter, pungent, hot, salt astringent, sour and such other substances of painful effect, which are devoured by the mother and consequently suffering produced all over the body, bound by membranes sheath [amnions] and in the outside surrounded by entrails, it lies in that cavity with its head bent towards the stomach and with its back and neck bent like a bow. Other than human beings, no other living beings have the faculty to know Him and to make amends through the right action and can realize the Supreme. Though we lead a very miserable life here but do not wish to get out from here, but again and again fall into the darkness of the world [external], where the *māyā* overtakes the being, giving wrong notion regarding the body as self, to be caught again in the wheel of *samsāra*. Therefore, the *Jīva* wishes to live here and get all the miseries with the help of mind that has given the access to the feet of the Lord *Viṣṇu.* When the *Jīva*, who is thus endowed with the knowledge and is ten-month old in the womb, remains, praising the Lord with his mind thus made up but the wind of birth suddenly propels him with a head downwards so that he may issue out of the womb. Thus, suddenly thrust out by the wind with his head downwards and in great distress, the *Jīva* gets out, full of pain, breathlessness and deprived of memory.

The individual is a bundle of actions; the actions that are fructified are experienced, exhausted and simultaneously earned for future. Fallen on the earth in a pool of blood and urine, the creature is in motion like a worm produced in it and weeps bitterly, the light of knowledge having gone, falls into the opposite state of darkness. Now coming into contact with people who do not know the mind of others, the creature is unable to refuse, what it does not want. It is helpless. It cannot even scratch its body when itching, can not sit or stand, can not resist the mosquitoes or flies and deprived of the knowledge that it had in the womb but only cry and cry.

The fruits of its previous actions keep it in bondage. How this *Jīva* can attain again the natural state by any other means than through the grace of the Lord but by virtue of the *Māyā*, the *Jīva* has lost its memory of his own true self and is wandering in the path of *samsāra* with the sufferings produced in it – the path in which he becomes fettered with heavy *karma* induced by the three *guṇas.*

The above treatise is to bring together all the different ways of transmigration, the plurality is due to the natural actions as well as of the rites combined with meditations that are enjoined by the scriptures. Rites lead to the world of manes and meditations as well as rites lead to the heaven. The topic to be expanded here is the knowledge of the results of rites and through that the *Śruti* wishes to enjoin here the meditation on the five fires, which is the means for getting access to the northern way. This is the highest result of rites.

The Ritual After the Birth of The Son

The child should be kept on the lap at the sacrificial fire. The oblation offered is a mixture of curd, clarified butter and is offered again and again, saying, "While growing in this house of mine [as the son], may I maintain a thousand people. May the goddess of fortune never depart with children and animals from his line! *Svāhā.* The vital force that is in me, I mentally transfer to you! *Svāhā.* If I have done anything too much or too little in the ceremony, may the all knowing beneficent fire just set it right for me, neither too much nor too little! *Svāhā.* Next putting the mouth close to the child's ear repeat three times 'speech, speech and speech'. Then the child should be fed with honey mixed with clarified butter with a strip, may be of gold, saying 'I put the earth into you, I put the sky into you, I put the heaven into you, I put the whole of earth, sky and heaven into you'. Then name is given 'you are Veda [knowledge]'. That is his secret name.

After handing over the child to mother, to be suckled, saying 'O Sarasvati, that breast of thine, which is stored with results is the sustainer of all, full of milk, obtainer of wealth and generous through which thou nourishest all who are worth of it - transfer that here to my wife for my babe to suck'. Then the mother is addressed thus 'you are the adorable like

Arundhati, the wife of sage Vaśiṣṭha, you have brought forth a male child with the help of me, who am a man. Be the mother of many sons, for you have given us a son'. Of him who is born as the child of a *Brāhmaṇa* with the particular knowledge, they say, 'you may exceed your father. You may reach the extreme limit of attainment through your splendor, fame and *Brhaminical power*'.

Ignorance (अविद्या - संसार दर्शनम्)

A journey from helplessness to another helpless state of condition is life. The young one gets the support of parents for the very existence. Parents' hands are his hands; their legs are his legs for moving about. There can be any reference since it is cyclic in order. When parents made him stable and able, one performs many deeds of rarity and achieves the impossible things, then quits the world as if all these were ends of all ends. World too has very short memory, the footprints on the sand, stay only until another wave sweeps that. Water becomes wave again and again, that has a form and one can give a name to it and also there is a big wave and small wave or any other type of nomenclature that suits us. The word and its contents are always at flux. They continuously go on changing from one condition to another condition. When we give name to a matter, this concept can go to conceive that this body is constantly on the path of birth and death. The death is in the form of destruction and replacement of every cell. What was yesterday the cell might have changed to waste. Every moment the cells are dying and get rejuvenated and this process has the time as its factor. The time is death because the time alone decides as to what ought to live and leave. Our breaths have been numbered on the scale of time and this time is proportionate, depending upon the enjoyment and suffering that one has to undergo based on *karma*. [The actions and the corresponding results]. This is what death; it is the reduction in the allotted joy and suffering. It is the destruction of vigour, energy and strength together, the capacity to enjoy as well as the pleasure store for the object of enjoyment as far as the individual is concerned.

Birth again goes to explain that every moment that is spent in action in any form gets accumulated towards the result [merit/demerit] for that particular life span and style, one is going to experience hereafter. So it must be clearly understood that our actions and reactions have two components, one is the benefit or result of the action and the other one is the brick for the future foundation, both go hand in hand. The individual is not given to know the differentiation. One can think in terms of the journey as we advance, when we approach some point, the way we had left behind. In this light we can see the modifications taking place in the body, the matter, irrespective of whether it is a body of even an incarnation, the same law applies to the body, whatever be the merit or demerit, on the anvil of the time. First the body exists in some form or the other. The body in the mother's womb is not allowed to exist beyond the time of life allotted to it. When the time comes, it is ejected out by natural forces to the perception of the world and a new state of existence is given, here the name is birth of the body, which is helpless, incapable of fulfilling its needs or protect itself, so the very survival of the body depends upon the parents.

The parents take care of the comfort and make available all the nourishments suitable to it. Thus, the body starts growing gradually to the stage where development is completed and thereafter the growth stops. Now the state of full-fledged form is reached and in that state of existence remain for certain time so that the full energy could be harnessed for fulfilment of all worldly enjoyments available at its credit. After some time, the reverse process of disintegration starts and declining from the peak to down hill fall begins. The dissipated energy tells on the vigour and health of the body and host of weaknesses and diseases descend, that were waiting to get a hold into the system and the whole system starts malfunctioning. Does this process continue forever? No. This too has its stipulated time and when that point is reached, it undergoes final disintegration and integration. The individual mass gets separated into its constituents to be combined with the respective elements.

This range of change/modifications is given the name of the six modifications of the body – the matter. The given body has done its functions for which it came into existence. The particular form of the body in question was too intended for the specific enjoyment or sufferings, the body in question is capable of the type it can afford to withstand it. One is entitled to enjoy the human pleasures, provided with a human body, not animal or plant body. This is how the Lord, who has all the knowledge of the aggregate and individual pleasure and pain in stock, that has to be exhausted, created the universe, [Subject – object.] and the bodies that are required. Everything goes according to the plan and not as an accident. There is no place for accident in nature's plan of creation.

Samsāra Born of Ignorance

- Ego that divides the *Jīvātma* and *Paramātma.*
- Doership and the enjoyer ship.
- Desires.
- Action – *karma.*
- Products of action – merits and demerits.
- Pleasure and pain – the reactions.
- Re-birth and death.

The ignorance causes error, the host of all sufferings and this error is also the bondage. Therefore, if the bondage has to go, the error must go and to get rid of the error, ignorance must go. To seek liberation, the ignorance must be replaced with the knowledge. The rope and snake example will make the meaning of ignorance, the miseries and tragedies born of error, clearer.

In semi-dark conditions, when one is not able to see clearly, a coiled rope cannot be made out. One is also aware how a snake looks like, as pre-conceived. Here under partial visibility or partial invisibility, the rope is seen like a snake. In fully lighted condition there is no problem as the rope is seen clearly. In full darkness also there is no problem, as even if it is a real snake cannot be seen. Ignorance is bliss. But here part of the phenomenal world is hidden [covered] – not known and also that part, which is known – not covered. In the statement "There is snake", "There is" is common, which is known as '*sāmānya amśa*', whereas the unreal snake is called '*anāvṛta amśa*' and the rope which is hidden is known as '*āvṛta amśa*'. The hidden part is real — the snake, which is unreal — mitya, replaces the ropeness — the specific feature of the object. We have in every error, two parts. One is real and the other unreal. We can see how these two features combined together created snake out of the rope, the cause of fear and misery.

Extending the same logic, we have a statement ***"I am samsāri"***, in which 'I am' is '*sāmānya amśa*' whereas the word '*samsāri*' is unreal part, the erroneous opinion. The covering of the statement, Brahman – the *Ātma* by the word '*samsāri*' appears as though real. At the dawn of the knowledge, the error is removed, just as the light makes the darkness to disappear and one finds the harmless rope where the snake was seen. One discovers that **"I am Brahman"** – the *Sat-chid-ānanda. Vedāntins* use the term '*avidya*' – ignorance and '*prakṛtī*' synonymous with *māyā* – for these confusions.

Precisely *Māyā stands* for cosmic illusion. *Māyā* is responsible for the contradictions in our thinking, on account of which alone Consciousness does not appear as the creator of the universe. Under the influence of ignorance *Ātma* is seen as *Jīva* or the individualized self. Ignorance is the one which makes the Absolute to appear as the relative or the One as many. The *Prakṛti* means *māyā*, the material out of which the universe has been created. The words *māyā*, ignorance, nature and matter are often interchanged.

Tamas is the veiling power that hides the true nature of a thing and makes it to appear something else than what really it is. This influence is seen in man in his ignorance, lassitude, dullness, inadvertence, and stupidity that deprives the man of right judgement or definite belief and keeps him in doubt and uncertainty. The *rajas* exerts its power of projecting many fantasies together with the veiling power. It is like hypnotic-spell – the delusion. *Rajas* and *Tamas* have opposing qualities, while *Sattva* strikes the balance between the two. *Sattva* is the giver of happiness and is the real friend of man in his effort to realize the Truth. Predominance of *Sattva* makes a man to feel detached to the world. *Sattva* keeps the other two *guṇas* under control. The three qualities [*guṇas*] of the *māyā* are exemplified to three robbers on the highway, who waylay men. The three waylaid a man in the forest. The robber *Tamas* wanted to destroy the man forever, but the robber *Rajas* stepped in and bound the hands and feet of the man, tied him to a tree and relieved him of all the belongings. The third robber, *Sattva* returned back after, to free the man from bondage, as it were, led him gently out of the forest and put him on the right path to his village. The robber *Satva* does not accompany the man out of forest; he too being a robber fears the consequences.

The *māyā* is a statement of fact in our general and relative life in this world of duality we have. The *māyā* is described as ***'aghaṭana ghaṭana paṭiyasi'*** making the impossible possible. Under its influence even an incarnation of God appears to forget his superhuman resplendence and acts like a common man on the street. *Māyā* also causes to contradict our actions and thoughts. For example, good is invariably followed by evil. The cause only decides the effect but still we attempt to do good for self and turn evil to others. This is *māyā*. Here a man robs his fellow men and then gives away his part or full wealth to the cause of philanthropy expecting eternal happiness.

Ego

The ego or *ahamkāra* is a virtue when it is subservient, means good to the self, to the society and to all beings. But when the same is supported by the ignorance, it is a dangerous and destructive tool. *Sadhu ahamkāra* is a means for liberation whereas evil *ahamkāra* cuts the very root and opens the floodgate of hell to its master, the owner. *Ahamkāra* tends to identify with the body, body-related relations, mind and mind-related projections. The body and mind do noble deeds as well as evil deeds and thus the attachment with these causes to bring good and bad products [effects]. It is denoted with the small letter 'i' which is slightly crooked and the individual too. But, capital, 'I' is used when related to the Total – the Infinite. In ordinary sense, all desires, impressions and lust hang upon the ego – the chief of the house – the body.

Normally, in childhood, it is not deep and effective but by the time one grows to adolescence, marries and gets entangled with achievements of various worldly desires, the ego gets rooted firmly and this world becomes more real. When the ego – *ahamkāra* asserts as "I am Brahman", it is cause for divinity in oneself and gets liberated from the miseries of the world but when it adopts itself with the fleshy physical body, it is the source for host of troubles and it is hard to come out of it. The ego – *ahamkāra* hides the knowledge of Self as the clouds hide the sun. It is very apt in ramifying long branches of "me, mine, you and thine" which is the very cause of afflictions and sorrow. The *māyā* means *ahamkāra* and the mind is another name of *ahamkāra*, the very world is *ahamkāra* and it wants to live in flesh, to eat flesh and to embrace flesh.

Ego has no standing of its own but simply fattened at others' cost or glory. One individual invited many guests for the house-warming ceremony of the house he had built new. Friends and well-wishers had gathered in strength and greeted for the achievement. All were in happy mood and the host with his family was upbeat. As a routine, one of the guests asked "How much did you pay for this?"

The reply from the host was "thirty lakhs".
The next question was "what is the extent of land?"
The reply was "it is a common property".
The question was "how about the floor?"
The reply was "no, it is the roof of the ground floor".
The question "how about the roof?"
The answer was "it is the floor for the building above".
The question "what about the walls"?
The reply was "it belongs to the neighbour".
The host "then what belongs to you?"
The reply was "the space".
The comment was "you could have had the space without paying thirty lakhs".

This is how 'ego' vanishes when it is subjected to systematic analysis. Here it may be noted that nothing belongs to one, who is celebrating the ownership/acquisition. Thus, the ego is a false notion – a mental modification without substance. Egotism breeds attachment; attachment leads to aversion. The result of these chain reactions is so tremendous that one starts clinging to life and suffers. A man achieves neither knowledge nor liberation as long as he has egotism. But all troubles come to an end when the ego dies.

This cannot be removed all at once but can only be reduced slowly and steadily. Even to say "I am Brahman" *ahamkāra* is needed but this has no capacity to bind but rather to free from the bondage, since 'Brahman is free' is the concept of Self-realization. Ego is developed through the thoughts in mind. The idea of 'I' brings the idea of time, space and other conceptual potencies with the environments and like a thread connects the sense organs. Ego is the corner stone of edifice of *Jīva* and on the basis of *buddhi* binds the man to the world. When one tries to analyze then the 'i' becomes a non-entity. The analysis should be on the line that this body cannot be "I" and even when some part of the body is cut or goes out of service, "I" remains always". Anyway, it is interesting to think on the subject and try to know what it is and from where it came and rests upon.

Action: *Karma*

Karma is inherent in Nature, which is constituted of the three *guṇas* – *Sattva*, *Rajas* and *Tamas*. But there is no *karma*, whatsoever in *Ātma*. The ignorant man is incapable of distinguishing between the action-ridden Nature and the actionless Self.

When two trains are standing side by side on the railway platform, a passenger in one of the trains fixes his gaze on the other train. When the other train moves, the man fancies that the train in which he is sitting moves. Likewise, the mobility of Nature is imposed on the immobile *Ātma*. Mistaking Nature for Ātma brings about egoism. Bondage persists as long as egoism lasts. The egoistic man thinks of himself as the doer, while actually he is not. Egoism and agency are the outcome of ignorance. All activities pertaining to bodily existence take place in the non-self. The Self is actionless. The knower of Self is, therefore, free from agency.

Desires

The desires are innumerable, insatiable and difficult to conquer. Enjoyment cannot bring in satisfaction. It is like pouring clarified butter into fire. Enjoyment increases, strengthens and aggravates the desire. The king Yayāti asked his sons to lend their youthfulness. Though his first four sons refused to part with their youthfulness, his youngest son Puru wholeheartedly accepted his father's old age in exchange for his youth and went to the forest. After enjoying the worldly pleasures for more than a thousand years, Yayāti realized and advised the lesson that there is no satiability from the sense pleasures. Even all the wealth and women may not be able to satisfy even a single man. —*P.P.*

Desire grown to the stature of greed is a destructive force and an enemy to all human beings. But the ignorant among them, who comes under its sway, holds it as a helpful friend. Whenever a setback and humiliation ensues from it, the destructive force of desire is momentarily detested as a treacherous factor in the make up of man. But this feeling runs away as quickly as it came. The unwary ignorant chooses to ally with it always. The wise man keeps no alliance but still it steals into his heart assuming innumerable forms, trying to allure him. It is, therefore, the constant foe of the wise.

Men are generally the victims of the subtle hidden desires. So long such subtle and hidden desires continue to be there unnoticed, one cannot enter into '*Nirvikalpa*' state. The desires arise in the mind and, therefore, it agitates the mind till one gets satisfaction through enjoyment. It is the ego that aggravates the desires. The desire calls for action and if there is an increase in the desires, the activities too increase. Thus, activity and desire move in a vicious circle. The nature of the desire depends upon the predominant *guṇa* of the individual. This division is explained through the legend:

"The three kinds of sons of Prajāpati lived with their father studying the Vedas – gods, men and demons. Having finished the study of Vedas, the gods said, "let your Honour speak to us". To them he spoke this syllable, "Da", and asked, "Do you understand?" "We understand," they said. "You said, control yourselves [dāmyata]. "Yes, you understand," Prajāpati said.

Then the men told him, "let your Honour speak to us." To them he spoke the same syllable "Da", and asked, "Do you understand?" They replied, "Yes, you said, be charitable [data]. "Yes" said Prajāpati.

Then to the demons also he spoke the same syllable "Da". And asked whether they too understood. The demons said in affirmative and said, "Yes, be compassionate – daydhvam". Thus, the same word 'Da' was understood in different ways by gods, men and demons. *—Bṛ V.ii.1-3*

All the desires happen unconditionally and the means of the happiness conditionally. This is explained herewith in the statements of Yājñavalkya. He said "Lo! The husband verily is dear not out of love for the husband but the husband is dear out of love for the self. Lo! The wife is verily dear not out of love for the wife, but the wife is dear out of love for the self. Same is the case with the sons and all other relations and relative things of the world". *—Bṛ II.iv.5*

Things are desired as long as it gives pleasure and when it ceases to give the pleasure, same things are not desired, it may be wife, husband, house and all other things. That is why, there is conditional desirability for the means of pleasure.

World of Men

Action cannot destroy ignorance, as it is not in conflict with ignorance. Knowledge alone destroys ignorance as light destroys dense darkness. Nights, days, fortnights, months, half years [the time taken for the passage of the sun from one solstice to another] and years roll on, yet the desire leaves not. In this world of doubt and delusion of darkness, pain and grief, nobody ever knows the result of his action, nor does he know his beginning or end; wearily does he go down the scale of creation and finds peace nowhere. The mankind is sick at heart and physically at dire distress. The sensual pleasures are eating into the vitals. None is being spared from the venoms. To add to it are the deplorable conditions of body and mind, which suffer from constant fever of unrest and its onslaughts. The search for external happiness continues which they never find. It is a mirage, which eludes all. Wealth, health, power and pleasure are so shortlived that they pass off in a flash and leave people confounded. Greater the indulgence, more diseased is the body, deeper the miseries and sufferings. Wonderful are the people who have come to believe that all the pleasure objects are imperishable for them.

- In the forest, lion kills tiger and tiger kills fox. In the water, big fishes live on smaller fishes and smaller ones live on the smallest. Powerful birds kill the weaker and smaller ones for their food. But the wonderful man kills all of them for pleasure and he is the most cruel. He patronizes the slaughterhouse and injures many animals while hunting but is afraid even of a prick of the injection needle on his body.
- The trees that provide shades help in protecting the ecological balance, give their sweet flowers and fruits selflessly but the selfish man cuts these very trees.
- While in mother's womb, hands and head down in utterly appalling condition is a rigorous penance, what sustains the baby is the constant prayer that in the new life he will ever remember his Creator. However, as soon he is born, all around him is the strange scene and novel objects. Beholding them all, he forgets the promise and becomes oblivious of his creator.

CHAPTER IV

Some More Rumblings

CHAPTER IV

Some More Rumblings

Religion and Rebirth

The religion and philosophy are inter-dependent. Philosophy without religion is like a barren woman. To be acceptable to the modern mind both of them need the support of the reason [Logic]. As far as the re-birth is concerned, it is the matrix of series of cause and effect and the final trace back is the Absolute, which has no cause, as it is the cause unto itself.

Therefore, the objective evolution to break the cycle is the Absolute. To make endeavour to that goal, perhaps one may need to assess oneself, the progress one has made so far and the distance yet to be made good. In this direction, we overview the milestones and review the point where we stand, to go over further.

Dualists

The nearness to the God is not realized, when we are dualists. God is the creator and ruler, has separate entity and form. The attributes are highly magnified with relation to the individual soul or *jīvātma*. As far as the dualists are concerned, God is all-powerful, all knowing and merciful. He is the efficient cause of the universe and uses *prakṛti* – nature as material for creation. According to this school, the human soul is eternal and potential in the nature, which manifests in the gross form, one after another based on its desires, tendencies and actions.

Human beings are supposed to obey the intention and instructions of the God to purify themselves from the impurities such as selfishness and other dark shades of the relative conducts. The liberation or the ultimate goal of the dualists is the heaven, which is the abode of the Lord, and free from the miseries of this world. In heaven, everything is pleasant and enjoyable. Moreover, those who led a virtuous life can live in the presence of the Lord, and those who were wicked are subjected to punishment of different types, through the institution known as hell and various fires of hell. God is like an ocean and the individual, the river and just as all rivers merge into the ocean ceaselessly, so also, the souls struggle to merge into Him.

Dualists worship the God, establishing worldly relation with Him just as friend, mother, father, husband, son etc. according to the individual's tendency. This humanly love for God gets transformed into divine love and devotion. Dualists conceive God as an emperor too and wish to be like a law-abiding subject, paying their own tributes for protection and sustenance, just as the relationship of a master-servant. According to them each one has a separate soul and that it always maintains its separate identity in this world and even in heaven. So the distance between God and oneself is like the individuals with each other.

The Qualified Non-Dualists

God is here, immanent, that is, the physical universe is His gross body as well as all the physical organs are His organs such as eyes, ears, nose and mouth, etc. The cosmic intellect, mind and ego are His intellect, mind and ego. He is the intelligent and material cause of the universe. He is one – the living beings in the universe – the whole and we are all the parts, so there is the relationship of whole and parts, between the God and individual beings.

The term qualified-non-dualism applies as the unity is qualified by variety. Though the souls, that is, the human and the universe are one, but still they consider themselves as a separate entity. The soul has mind, intellect, sense, energy and memory. At the time of death, the soul contracts just as the tortoise withdraws itself into its shell and expands at the time of birth, which were in potential form. Sri Rāmānujācārya is the exponent of qualified-non-dualist religion philosophy as they are closer to the dualists in comparison, talked about in the previous pages.

Non-Dualists

The non-dualists are the closest to the God or we can say that they identify themselves with the God Himself and claim that He – the *Īśvara* and [he] – the *Jīva*, both are Consciousness. The only line that separates them is the adjunct. According to this school, the ego or the individual soul is the changing receptacle of a still subtler substance, which does not change and eternal, called by the name *Ātma*, which is the unconditional reality in all the living beings. It is to be noted here that the ego is the unconditional reality of the universe, the Brahman, the Consciousness, is the all-pervading spirit, the very Absolute. The *Ātman* or Self is sexless, the real, is not based on created and creator or part and whole relationship as discussed before. All distinctions dissolve into one reality, which is unchangeable, eternal, formless and beyond the time, space and quality. The relation is further defined as the reflection or image of the Self-effulgent light of the God, *Bimba-pratibimba* relationship.

Nearness is illustrated through this prayerful statement:

"O Lord! When I think of my body, I am thy servant and thou are my master. When I look at my soul, I am thy part and thou art the one, stupendous whole but when I realize my true nature I am divine and one with thee, the Absolute Spirit. Such is my conception of my relation to thee".

This explains our nearness to the God, who is the Absolute cause in our discussion of cause and effect relation law that goes to establish the intermediary and Absolute causes.

"That is this and this is that".

The Resurrection and Re-Incarnation

These two are technical terms and do not fit in the same slot and common understanding. The resurrection was coined to the faith of Christianity and is an expression of the immortality of the body [such as the rising of the Jesus Christ from the tomb or the rising of all the dead at the last judgement]. It is the doctrine of the Sadducees, the Jewish ideas, professed ceremonies, rituals and beliefs after the death of Jesus. The doctrine of the resurrection of the dead, of reward and punishment after death and the belief in angels and spirits became the cardinal principle of the new Christian sect. The Zoroastrians believed that the soul of the dead hovers around the body for three nights and does not depart for the other world until dawn of the third night. They also believe in resurrection of not only the body but the soul also by an act of miracle, which applied to Jesus.

Jesus never mentioned about the kind of resurrection whether of body or soul but his disciples took it to mean the body that is the reappearance of his physical form. Again Christ was the first born to resurrect and was preached that those who have belief in him too, shall attain to it. The concept of miraculous resurrection is attended with the belief that the individual soul does not exist before birth and also the creation out of nothing. It is now clear that resurrection has nothing to do with our study of transmigration, based on the solid foundation of cause and effect. It is not meant to say that resurrection is an aberration, but let be the means for further enquiry by those who believe this as good. It is good initially to consolidate the faith for maturity, for spiritual practices at later date. We must give it the benefit of evolution, to those who are in search of the proper base to land and go further.

The reader may be probably in a mind to mind the scope of reincarnation, which is very often used in the same sense as rebirth or transmigration or the cycle of birth and death, though there is a subtle difference to the word 'reincarnation' with reference to other similar expressions. The confusion or mix up is due to the prefix 're' which conveys the idea of repetition as the word rebirth means. Let us take the world. Incarnation is the propriety of the master soul or the perfect soul, which does not need any improvement or refinement, since it is already Infinite, bigger than biggest, purer than purest, smaller than smallest, formless, beyond the causation, being the Absolute cause.

Incarnation applies to taking a form [manifestation], coming down to perception level, so as to be seen, understood and followed as an ideal to be attained through birth [evolution], that accords purification in subtle level of existence. When we say it is beyond causation, it means that its appearance is not to work out the previous *karma*, as it is taking birth, but on free will and to remain unattached to any action, just as sunlight. The sunlight illumines both the dirt and the beautiful one, but does not become dirty or glorious, because of the borrowed glory. The light is also not partial to any object and illumines all objects equally. If someone does not harness this energy, it is his choice and the sun neither gets displeased nor pleased with it in any way.

The Lord has created this universe and made certain laws to be followed, at the gross and subtle level of the universe, both at macro and micro levels of existence in order to fulfill the very objective of the creation or manifestation. What happens often, after some time, is that the regulating institutions or noble instincts get debased, as this is also the law of nature, which arises due to conflict in intent and purpose. Some of the variations are designed to be self-aligning to maintain the equilibrium, whereas some miss the target and the path becomes long to return. Here it becomes necessary for the Lord to correct the course as the interference becomes painful to the beings. At this point, the Lord takes the form of his choice, appropriate to the situation so as to establish the law of truth and justice. Since this process has to be reviewed and corrected regularly, after the lapse of certain duration from time to time, He assumes the work unto Himself, which explains the prefix 're'. So is the reincarnation. When the injury fails to yield to immunity system, surgery must be carried out. Both are the systems of treatment and they are valid for the embodied souls.

The rebirth relates to the human beings, the embodied ones, and the evolving souls. There is limitation in the adjuncts of the beings and *Īśvara*, as far as the prowess, purpose and functions are concerned. This limitation of the *upādhis* is the only difference, otherwise the Awareness is the one and the same thing. The adjuncts only decide the address and, in fact, the address is only to the adjuncts and not to the spirit. Therefore, it is imperative to maintain proper identification thereto. When an object is good, we must not say 'very good'; otherwise for the 'very good' object we have to use superlative degree and superlative will have no suitable vocabulary.

The intended idea to be conveyed here is that reincarnation and rebirth are not one and the same expression, though extensively used; both have mortal body but their capacities and purpose are different.

Heredity and Evolution

What is the role played by heredity passage and transmigration? The believers of heredity deny the pre and post existence of the soul and accordingly they say that the offsprings not only resemble their parents but also inherit other qualities of the individual such as mental faculties and impressions both in human existence and also in animals. They define that the heredity is supply and a simple continuity of growth. Dr. Weismann believes that the germ plasm contains the potentiality of all the tendencies which are developed in an individual, passes through generation to generation and at particular condition of the life, it expresses as tendencies and characteristics of the life.

It is refined to the extent that the germ cells are transmitted through the channel of the parents and the tendencies are attributed to the germ cells, which existed but are not created by parents themselves. The difficulty in accepting these or similar concepts is that they are not able to explain the disparity in unity as well as the advent of prodigy. Those who are against this theory, express their concern such as the creation of individual organism and that thus transmitted by the parents for retransmission. Also the capacity and quality of the germ cell on scientific viewpoint is debatable.

Let us assume that the heredity is formed not in the body but relates to the mind, before birth, that is, the individual soul or the embodied soul after death mingles with similar tendencies, as the proverb "birds of same feather flock together". Thus, coming together is not common in all aspects but only limited identity. The individual soul evolves, but continues to be attracted by the link of generation. This assumption takes care of the theory of the cause and effect – continuity of tie – the transmigration and at the same time, maintains the bond of the family, a heredity that need not be in equality in manifestation. It is simply for the sake of discharging the debt that one owes of the previous birth. Thus the appearance of the prodigy and inequalities in mental and physical tendencies on the unit may not disturb in any way and the universal law of *karma* can also be accommodated predominantly in its full glory and effectiveness.

The law of causation through evolution operates to progressive development, unfolding and refinement, from simplicity to complexity. The evolution of man is not a direct or a one-shot result, but has gradually come from series, may be the animal life even. The necessity of evolution demands three principal conditions – the tendency to vary, the tendency of environmental influence, that is, the natural selection and the struggle for existence or survival. The animal tendencies are the same as that of man except the developed intelligence and senses that crown the man as an epitome of the creation; some may call this as a civilized society of man and others as social animal.

The higher nature of man is symbolized through love, truthfulness, mercy, selflessness, desire to help others and forgiveness, etc. These are moral and spiritual nature, which is of filling as much as possible rather than survival of the fittest that must have developed from the desire of maximum – the quality and continuity, which are the expressions of the satisfaction and must have existed in bio-plasma in latent or potential. This part has reference to the point raised against heredity tendency, doubted by the opponents of the same. The expression of accommodation is natural, thus the moral law. It is a sort of defence mechanism, developed through self-pity and helplessness that comes in the passage of time, where the propensity to enjoy or to have is still active. It is a form of natural involution, later occupied the place of justice – common defence system.

To accept the slumber and potentiality, the illustration is that of the dry seed, that sprouts after thousands of years, at appropriate condition, which was found in the hands of the Egyptian mummy. The concept of evolution that the in-filling of nature means that nothing is superceded to the individual soul from outside as potential or germ is already there but development depends upon the suitable condition when appropriate point/stage in process is reached. There is priority and sequence in every transmigration or development; one has to be over before the start of the next. We understand that why fruits do not appear before the appearance of the leaves, because the leaves need to sustain themselves as well as the tree before the tree becomes capable of yielding fruits, as it has to harness certain energy for it.

The Vedānta on evolution says that the end and aim of evolution is the attainment of perfection. The animal life reached its perfection in human form; the mental disposition is matching its journey to Absolute, which is the cause of all causes, the moral and spiritual. It has many stages in the subtle body. The evolution is the process where the soul is involved. The heredity is the cycle; whereas the evolution is the enrichment, both combined together make some sense and also comforts, the supporter of the law of heredity. Thus, we can make out the compromise that the heredity and evolution are the part of transmigration in the same sense or other, from the fact that every law of nature is interwoven and complementary. The natural law supports each other and does not destroy or stand in isolation from each other.

Now comes a very interesting question, that question which is generally known as birth. Sometimes people get frightened at that idea and superstition is so strong that even some thinking men believe that they are the outcome of nothing and then, with the grandest logic, try to deduce the theory that although they have come out of zero, they will be eternal. Those that come out of zero will certainly have to go back to zero. Neither you nor anyone present has come out of zero. We have been existing eternally and will exist and there is no power under the sun or above the sun, which can undo your or any existence or send us back to zero. Now this idea of rebirth is not a frightening idea, but is most essential for the moral well being of the human race. It is the only logical conclusion that thoughtful men can arrive at. If you are going to exist in eternity hereafter, it must be that you had existed through eternity in the past. It cannot be otherwise. We will discuss few objections that are generally brought against the theory.

As it is, you and I are the effect, the result of all the infinite past, which is tacked on. When a great ancient sage, a seer, or a prophet of old, who came face to face with the truth, says about immortality of the soul, these modern men stand up and say, "Oh he was a fool!" They object, "If I am of the past, I must remember that. Just as after sleep, when I get up, I remember all that I had before going to sleep". But just use another name, "Huxley says it, or Tyndall"; then it must be true and they take it for granted. In place of ancient superstitions, they have erected modern superstitions, in place of the old umpire, they have installed new reign of modern science. So we see that this objection as to memory is not valid and that is about the only serious objection that is raised against this theory. Although we have seen that it is not necessary for the theory of rebirth, that there shall be memory of past lives, yet at the same time, we are in a position to assert that there are instances which show that this memory does come, and that each one of us will get back this memory in that life in which, one will become free. Then alone you will find that this world is but a dream; then alone you will realize the Soul and understand that you are but an actor and the world is a stage; then alone will the idea of non-attachment come to you with the power of thunder; then all this thirst for enjoyment, this clinging on to life and this world will vanish forever; then the mind will see clearly as daylight how many times all these existed for you, how millions of times you had fathers and mothers, sons and daughters, husbands and wives, relatives and friends, wealth and power came and went, how many times you were on the topmost crest of wave and how many times you were down at the bottom of despair! When memory will bring all these to you, then alone will you stand as a hero and smile when the world frowns upon you. Then alone will you stand up and say, "I care not for thee even, O Death; what terrors hast thou for me?" This will come to all.

Are there any arguments, any rational proofs for this rebirth? So far we have been giving the negative side, arguments to disprove that the memory of the past are not valid. Is there any positive ground? Yes, there are positive and most valid ones, too. No other theory except that of rebirth accounts for the wide divergence that we find between man and man in their powers to acquire knowledge.

First, let us consider the process by means of which knowledge is acquired. Say, I go into the street and happened to see a dog. How do I say that it is a dog? I refer it to my mind, and in my mind are groups of all my past experiences, arranged and pigeonholed, as it were. As soon as a new impression comes, I take it up and refer it to some of the pigeonholes, and as soon as I find a group of the same impressions already existing, I place in that group and I am satisfied. I know it is a dog, because it coincides with the impressions already in the mind. When I do not find the cognates of this new experience inside, I become dissatisfied. This state of the mind is called 'ignorance'. The cognate of an impression already there, is called 'knowledge'. When one apple fell, men became dissatisfied. Then they found the group. That all apples fell, the knowledge is called "gravitation". Now we see that without a fund of already existing experiences, any new experience would be impossible, for there would be nothing to which to refer to the new impressions. So if, as some of the European philosophers think, a child came into the world with what they call *tabula rasa*, such a child would never attain to any degree of intellectual power, because he would have nothing to which to refer his new experiences. We see that the power of acquiring knowledge varies in each individual, and this shows that each one of us has his own fund of knowledge. Knowledge can only be got in one way, the way of experience. If we have not experienced it in this life, we must have experienced it in other lives. How is that the fear of death is everywhere? There is an old explanation [I should hardly dignify it by such name]. It is called instinct. Instinct is specific in every type of body that comes as expression in being. There is difference between the instincts of human beings, animals, birds, reptiles and water born species such as fish, etc. Now there is some complication if we identify the memory with the body. It goes to speak that the previous body too was of the present to imbibe the past into the present as that has gone to its constituents. Therefore, it can only belong to the soul that is the reflected Consciousness from the subtle body in which all the sense organs and mind have been resolved at the time of discarding the body. In the light of the concept of knowledge or memory "we have our own fund of knowledge". We see that the instinct is involved reason. What we call instinct in man or animal must, therefore, be involved, degenerated, voluntary actions and the voluntary actions are impossible without the experience.

The knowledge such as fear of death, the duckling taking to water etc., are all due to experience and all such involuntary actions have become instincts due to the past experiences. Now the instinct-experience relationship goes to establish that there is continuity of living experiences, that is the rebirth.

What makes the little chicken just out of the egg afraid to die? How is it that as soon a duckling hatched by a hen comes near water, it jumps into it and swims? It never swam before nor saw anything swim. People call it instinct. It is a big word, but it leaves us where we were before. Let us study the phenomenon of instinct. A child begins to play on the piano. At first, she must pay attention to every key she is fingering, and she goes on and on for months and years, the playing becomes almost involuntary, instinctive. What was first done with conscious will, does not require later on effort of the will. This is not yet a complete proof. One half remains, and that is that almost all the actions which are now instinctive can be brought under the control of the will. Each muscle of the body can be brought under the control. This is perfectly well known. So the proof is complete by this double method, that what we call now instinct is degeneration of voluntary actions; therefore, if the analogy applies to the whole creation, if all nature is uniform, then what is instinct in lower animals, as well as in men, must be the degeneration of will.

Applying the law we dwelt upon under macrocosm, that each involution presupposes an evolution and each evolution an involution, we see that instinct is involved reason. What we call instinct in men or animals must, therefore, be involved, degenerated, voluntary actions and voluntary actions are impossible without experience. Experience started that knowledge and that knowledge is there. The fear of death, the duckling taking to the water and all involuntary actions in human being, which have become instinct are the results of past experiences. So far we have proceeded very clearly and so far the latest science is with us. But here comes one more difficulty. The latest scientific men are coming back to the ancient sages and so far as they have done so, there is perfect agreement. They admit that each man and each animal is born with a fund of experience and that all these actions in the mind are the result of past experience. "But what", they ask, "is the use of saying that that experience belongs to the soul? Why not say it belongs to the body, and the body alone? Why not say it is hereditary transmission?" This is the last question. Why not say that all experiences with which I am born is the resultant effect of all the past experiences of my ancestors." The sum total of the experience from the little protoplasm up to the highest human being is in me, but it has come from body to body in the course of hereditary transmission. Where will the difficulty be? This question is very nice and we admit some part of this hereditary transmission. How far? As far as furnishing the materials. We, by our past actions, conform ourselves to a certain birth in a certain body and the only suitable material for that body comes from the parents who have made themselves fit to have that soul as their offspring.

The simple hereditary takes for granted the most astonishing proposition without any proof, that mental experience can be recorded in matters, that mental experience can be involved in matter. When I look at you, in the lake of my mind, there is a wave. That wave subsides, but it remains in fine form, as an impression. We understand a physical impression remaining in the body. But what proof is there for assuming that the mental impression can remain in the body, since the body goes to pieces? What carries it? Even granting it were possible for each mental expression to remain in the body, that every impression, beginning from the first man down to my father, was in my father's body, how could it be transmitted to me? Through the bioplasmic cell? How could that be? Because the father's body does not come to the child in toto. The same parents may have number of children; then from this theory of hereditary transmission, where the impression and the impressed [that is to say, material] are one, it rigorously follows that by birth of every child, the parents must lose a part of their own impressions, or, if the parents should transmit the whole of their impressions, then after the birth of the first child, their minds would be a vacuum.

Again, from where and how have the infinite amount of impressions from all time have entered the bioplasmic cell? This is the most impossible position and until these psychologists can prove how and where those impressions live in the cell and what they mean by a mental impression sleeping in the physical cell, their position cannot be taken for granted. So far it is clear then, that this impression is in the mind, that the mind comes to take its birth and rebirth and uses the material, which is most proper for it and that the mind, which has made itself fit for only a particular kind of body, will have to wait until it gets that material. This we understand. The theory then comes to this, that there is hereditary transmission so far as furnishing the material to the soul is concerned. But the soul migrates and manufactures body after body and each thought we think and each deed we do, is stored in it in fine forms, ready to spring up again and take new shape. When I look at you, a wave rises in my mind. It dives down, as it were and becomes finer and finer, but it does not die. It is ready to spring up again as a wave in the shape of memory. So all these impressions are in my mind and when I die, the resultant force of them will be upon me.

Again a ball is here and each one of us takes a mallet in his hands and strikes the ball from all sides; the ball goes from point to point in the room and when it reaches the door, it flies out. What does it carry out with it? The resultant of all these blows that will give it, its direction. So what directs the soul when the body dies? The resultant, the sum total of all the works it has done, of the thoughts it has thought. If the resultant is such that it has to manufacture a new body for further experience, it will go to those parents who are ready to supply it with suitable material for that body. Thus, from body to body it will go sometimes to heaven and back again to earth becoming a man or some lower animal. This way it will go on until it has finished its experience and completed the circle. It then knows its own nature, knows what it is and ignorance vanishes, its powers become manifest, it becomes perfect; no more is there any necessity for the soul to work through physical bodies, nor is there any necessity for the soul to work through finer or mental bodies. It shines in its own light and is free, no more to be born, no more to die.

We will not go now into the particulars of this. But I will bring before you one more point with regard to this theory of rebirth. It is the one theory that advances the freedom of human soul. It is the one theory that does not lay the blame of all our weaknesses upon somebody else, which is a common human fallacy. We do not look at our own faults; the eyes do not see themselves, they see the eyes of everybody else. We human beings are very slow to recognize our own weaknesses, our own faults, so long as we can lay the blame upon somebody else. Men, in general, lay all the blame of life on their fellowmen, or failing that, on God or they conjure up a ghost, and say it is fate. Where is fate and who is fate? We reap what we sow. We are the makers of our own fate. None else has the blame, none has the praise. The wind is blowing; those vessels whose sails are unfurled, catch it and go forward on their way, but those which have their sails furled, do not catch the wind. Is it the fault of the wind? Is it the fault of the merciful father, whose wind of mercy is blowing without ceasing, day and night, whose mercy knows no decay, is it His fault that some of us are happy and some unhappy? We make our own destiny. His sun shines for the weak as well as for the strong. His wind blows for all the saints and sinners alike. He is the Lord of all, the father of all, merciful and impartial. Do you mean to say that He, the Lord of creation, looks upon the petty things of our life in the same light as we do? What a degenerate idea of God that would be! We are like little puppies, making life-and-death struggles here and foolishly thinking that even God himself will take it as seriously as we do. He knows what the puppies' play means. Our attempts to lay the blame on Him, making Him the punisher and rewarder are only foolish.

Karma Yoga and Transmigration

The student of the Gita may be pondering over lot on transmigration status, in the light of '*karma-yoga and karma-sanyāsa*'. If one feels that he never gave a thought about it, then it is desirable to think about it, as there is no other important problem in the world than to know about it, which demands priority. *Karma yoga* is the activity with all the intent and content, but without the expectation of a particular end result, that is supposed to follow the undertaking, the specific understanding. However, we see that not an atom moves without motive. All causes have their own effects and all effects have their causes inherent in it. The actions are good or bad because of its attendant intentions, the detachment and attachment. The action by itself is neither good nor evil, but becomes so when one's specific desire that motivates it. Desire is the one, which ties one with the wheel of *samsāra.* When the desire is removed the binding rope is burnt, remains with the mark of twist but without the strength to bind. Therefore the *Karma* of *karma yoga* has to be attended to, unmindful of the fruits thereof.

Now we will talk about the technique that is to be imbibed while doing action to convert the *karma* into *karma yoga.* The mind must be convinced that all the activities that are being carried out are the doings of the Lord and the individual self is merely a cog in the wheel, or the handmaid of the God. The action should be performed for the sake of *yajña* alone; free from attachment as it is an act of sacrifice and self-dedication, which is the inviolable law of the nature. Selfless service, a disinterested one, for the general welfare is adoration of the Lord, thus increasing the wealth of the country. Action is done for the sake of action alone with an attitude of duty towards the Lord, country and society. When all these thoughts are put behind the action, the action becomes inaction as far as the individual's *karma* is concerned and that man is a *karma yogi* of Bhagavad-Gita.

Again the actions are done, to be an example and inspiration for those, who may follow the suit afterwards, which becomes the path to be followed and as offerings to the God as worship with the flower. The result, which follows, is to be accepted as '*prasād*', the remnants of the oblations offered in the fire and this attitude is recommended for the *karma-yoga.* The comparison between *karma-yoga and karma-sanyāsa,* is that *karma-yoga* provides a wide experience to perfection, whereas *karma-sanyāsa* is deprived of such experiences, the passage through evolution.

What are the functionary elements in *karma-sanyāsa*? The *karma-sanyāsa,* which culminates in *Jñāna* – knowledge is known by the name of *karma-sanyāsa.* It is the theory and practice, which ought to be related, and interdependent to each other that the *karma-yoga* is *karma-sanyāsa.* To make it clearer, it is the right understanding that leads to right doing and right doing brings the right knowledge. This is the interchangeability between them. To be more precise, *Sanyāsa* is the renunciation of *sańkalpa*, which is inoperative for practice of the *yoga.* This makes the *sanyāsa, sańkalpa and karma-yoga* identical.

Deep meditation is the *yogi's* activity to sublimity of the self that is the way of performing the external work to perfection. The self-discipline is the means for self-control, which is consolidation of the mind and senses, the state of equilibrium or establishment into one's own self. The *sanyāsa-yoga* of fifth chapter is meant for active life of house-holder with internal detachment, which is known as '*Vidvat sanyāsa*' for purification of the mind to enshrine therein values and virtues and not *āśrama-sanyāsa.* It is followed with varieties of disciplines for regulating and balancing the life.

The reflection of the chapters 3, 5 and 6 of Bhagavad Gita on *karma-yoga, vidvat-sanyāsa and sadhana* are the topics of enquiry of *Jīva* [*tvam pada vicāra*]. That does not liberate one, but one improves his mental health, so the action of the body is not owned by the mind, which is a normal condition for the action. The man becomes *sātvic* predominant. So, when he is still governed by the law of cause and effect, the cause is noble and so the result too. The chain, whether it is made of iron or gold, is a chain, which binds the man to *karma.* The individual is subjected to be born in rewarding status, higher *loka* or maybe as gods or angels. After enjoying the higher life, when the effect is exhausted, returns back to the world of mortality. Vividly and beautifully described here is the transmigratory journey to heaven and back. The kite soars high up in the sky and falls back, when the string gets snapped somewhere according to the wind and gravitational forces.

ते तं भुक्त्वा स्वर्गलोकं विशालं क्षीणे पुण्ये मर्त्यलोकं विशन्ति ।
एवं त्रयी धर्ममनुप्रपन्ना गतागतं कामकामा लभन्ते ॥

"Having enjoyed the vast world of heaven, they return to the world of mortals on the exhaustion of their merits; thus abiding by the injunctions of the Vedas, desiring objects of desires they go and come". —*BG-IX-21*

The message is clear that *karma-yogi* is not exempted from the process of the retirement from one world to the other but only a *Jñāni*, the liberated soul [*Jīva*]. The *karma-yogi* retains the ego of 'doership'. With that very ego he offers the actions to the Lord or serve the society and becomes the torchbearer. So long as there is duality one cannot be freed from the birth and death relationship, the law of transmigration of the embodied soul.

Appendix

Instance of Past Memory

Reproduced hereunder a personal experience of Swami Satprakashananda of R.K. Math in his book titled "How is a man reborn?"

It may not be out of place to record from personal knowledge an authentic case of intuitive memory of past life. In 1935, when I was in New Delhi, I heard from a reliable friend, a teacher of Sanskrit in a high school, that a Brahmin girl of nine, Shanti Devi by name, who had been living with her parents in the old city, had memories of her past life since she had been a child. The secretary of the local Y.M.C.A. personally requested me to investigate the matter and ascertain the truth. But because of my preoccupation as the leader of the Ramakrishna Ashram in New Delhi, I could not take up the investigation. Not long after that I had to leave the city to make arrangements for my journey to the United States.

I gathered from different sources that since the girl had been five years old, she would remark from time to time with regard to certain food and dress, 'I have eaten this before, 'I have put on this before'. The mother paid little attention to the child's prattle. But as she grew up she spoke more definitely of her experiences in past life. She often asserted that she had lived in Mathura [a city about 150 miles to the south-east of Delhi], that her husband was a cloth merchant, that she remembered his name but would not give it out [because an orthodox Hindu woman does not as a rule utter the husband's name]. A grand uncle elicited from her the name and address of the husband, who was not a Brahmin, and who even came to Delhi when the case was related to him. He was accompanied by his son, who was one year older than Shanti Devi. As she saw the son she was deeply moved.

It was known upon enquiry that the mother of this boy died in a hospital in Mathura in 1925, shortly after giving birth to the son. Shanti Devi was born in Delhi in 1926. To verify the case, a party of about ten noteworthy citizens, including the editor of a local daily paper, a commissioner of Delhi Municipality and a college professor, went by train to Mathura accompanied by Shanti Devi, who had never been there before in this life. They discovered that Shanti Devi was well acquainted with the place and knew many details of the house where she claimed to have lived in her past life. She also visited her former parents and had no difficulty in finding the house where they lived even then.

This is to show that rebirth retains past memory too – the topic talks about the validity of rebirth in certain circumstances.

References

1. A history of western philosophy.
   By Bertrand Russell – Simm & Schuster, New York.
2. Outlines of Indian philosophy.
   By Hiriyanna – Motilal Banarsidas, New Delhi.
3. Indian Philosophy & Religion.
   By Bibhu Padhi, D.K. Print World, New Delhi.
4. The Doctrine of Karma.
   By Swami Abhedananda, Ramakrishna Publications.
5. Bṛhadāraṇyaka Upaniṣad.
   Translated by Swami Madhavananda, R.K. Publications.
6. Bhagavad-Gita.
   By Swami Chidbhavananda, R.K. Publications.
7. Life after death.
   By Swami Vivekananda, R.K.Publication.
8. Śvetāśvatara Upaniṣad.
   Translation by Swami Gambhīrānanda, Advaita Ashrama.
9. Tradition on Occultism.
   By M.P. Pandit, Sterling Publishers, New Delhi.
10. Upadeśa Sāhasrī.
    By Śrī Śaṅkarācārya, R.K. Publications.

Glossary

Advaita	Non-duality; a school of Vedānta philosophy teaching oneness of God, soul and universe.
Adhiṣṭhānam	Substratum.
Agnihotra	A vedic sacrifice in which oblations are offered to the Fire-god.
Ahaṁkāra	Ego or 'I' consciousness; one of the functions of the inner organ.
Ajñāna	A term in Vedānta philosophy meaning ignorance, individual or cosmic.
Ākāśa	The first of the five material elements that constitutes the universe.
Ānanda	Bliss.
Annamayakośa	The gross physical sheath.
Asura	Demon.
Ātma	The Self, or the soul; denotes also the supreme soul.
Avidya	A term of Vedānta philosophy meaning ignorance.

Brahmaloka	The plane of Brahma, roughly corresponding to the highest heaven of the dualistic religions, where fortunate souls repair after death and enjoy spiritual communion with the Personal God.
Brahman	The Absolute; the Supreme reality of Non-dualistic Vedanta.
Buddhi	The determinative faculty of the mind, which makes decisions; sometimes translated as intellect.
Dharma	Righteousness, duty.
Golakam	Physical organ.
Guṇa	Qualities of the nature.
Guru	Spiritual teacher.
Īśvara	Personal God.
Jīva	The individual soul.
Jñāna	Knowledge of reality.
Karma	Action in general; duty; ritualistic worship.
Kośa	Sheath or covering. According to Vedānta philosophy, there are five Kośas.

Liṅga	
Manomaya Kośa	The sheath of the mind.
Mantra	Holy Sanskrit text.
Māyā	A term of Vedānta philosophy denoting ignorance obscuring the vision of Reality; the cosmic illusion.
Mokśa	Liberation.
Nirguṇa Brahman	Brahman without attributes.
Pralaya	Deluge.
Prakṛti	Primordial nature; the material substratum of the creation.
Prārabdha karma	Action done in a previous life which has begun to bear fruit in the present life.
Purāṇas	Books of Hindu mythology.
Saguṇa Brahman	The Absolute conceived as the Creator, Preserver and Destroyer of the universe.
Samskāra	Culture.
Saṁsāra	The world of change and becoming; the relative world.
Śruti	The Vedas.
Śrāddha	Ceremony relating to ancestors of three generations.

Upādhi	A term of Vedānta philosophy denoting a limitation imposed upon the self or upon Brahman through ignorance.
Vāsana	Impressions.
Yajña	A fire ritual.
Yogabhrṣṭa	A man who has fallen from his goal.